7   Lady Frances Vane Tempest ————— Sir John Spencer-Churchill
7th Duke of Marlborough KG PC
1822– 1883

8   George Spencer-Churchill ———— 1) Lady Albertha Hamilton   Lord Randolph ———— Jennie Jerome
8th Duke of Marlborough   2) Lilian Hammersley   Spencer-Churchill
1844–1892

                                                 Sir Winston Churchill KG PC

9   Sir Charles Spencer-Churchill ———— 1) Consuelo Vanderbilt
9th Duke of Marlborough KG PC   2) Gladys Deacon
1871–1934

10   John Albert Spencer-Churchill ———— 1) Hon. Mary Cadogan
10th Duke of Marlborough   2) Laura Charteris
1897–1972

11   George John Vanderbilt Spencer-Churchill ———— 1) Susan Hornby
11th Duke of Marlborough   2) Tina Livanos
1926–2015   3) Rosita Douglas

12   Charles James Spencer-Churchill ———— 1) Rebecca Few Brown
12th Duke of Marlborough   2) Edla Griffiths
1955–

                    George John Spencer-Churchill
Marquess of Blandford
1992–

For Algie — Ed
with love
Milu

THE CHURCHILL
WHO SAVED BLENHEIM

Published in 2019 by Unicorn,
an imprint of Unicorn Publishing Group LLP
5 Newburgh Street, London
W1F 7RG

www.unicornpublishing.org

A catalogue record for this book is available from the British Library

ISBN 978-1-912690-22-0

THE CHURCHILL
WHO SAVED BLENHEIM

The Life of Sunny, 9th Duke of Marlborough

MICHAEL WATERHOUSE
& KAREN WISEMAN

Dedicated to four generations of Spencer-Churchills here
photographed in the Italian Garden at Blenheim Palace c. 1958.

From left to right: Robin Muir, Lady Elizabeth Spencer-Churchill,
Hugo Waterhouse, Ed Russell, Consuelo, the 10th Duke of Marlborough,
Lady Caroline Waterhouse, Lady Rosemary Muir.
Children in the cart from left to right: Robert Spencer-Churchill,
Alexander Muir, Michael Waterhouse, Elizabeth Waterhouse.

Contents

It is with great pride that I welcome this book on the life of my great grandfather, Sunny, 9th Duke of Marlborough. For a man so pivotal to the history of Blenheim it is surprising that so little has been written about him, except indirectly through the unfairly disparaging eyes of his two wives.

No custodian has done more for this glorious World Heritage Site since its completion than the 9th Duke of Marlborough, with a possible exception of the 4th Duke. At the end of the nineteenth-century Blenheim was laid low, following the excesses of a number of my ancestors. Sunny saw it as his duty to save his family home and as such participated in maybe the most celebrated 'arranged' marriage the modern world has ever witnessed. The resulting financial settlement was put to good use at Blenheim, albeit at great personal cost to his own happiness.

As my father the 11th Duke used to say, 'the never ending battle for Blenheim' continues, but thanks to the 9th Duke`s legacy we are winning. A century later I would like to think that my great grandfather would be proud of the current state of the Palace and the Estate and that he would marvel at the work of my professional management team in executing improvements and maintenance on a daily basis. Blenheim has been transformed over the last fifty years from a quasi-feudal ducal estate into a sophisticated and highly successful commercial enterprise. It was Sunny, 9th Duke of Marlborough, who created the platform for this transformation and in the process saved Blenheim for his family, the nation and the hundreds of thousands of visitors from around the world who come to witness its splendour every year.

It gives me great personal satisfaction that this book has been co-written by two authors so closely associated with my family and Blenheim. The biographer Michael Waterhouse is not only my first cousin, but the 9th Duke`s great grandson and grew up among the family he describes so well. Karen Wiseman was for many years the Head of Education and so has unparalleled knowledge of the research material she has used so deftly. Between them they have created a record of a remarkable period in my family`s and our nation`s history.

Charles James Spencer-Churchill, 12th Duke of Marlborough
Blenheim Palace
May 2019

Prologue

January 1901

In the New Year of 1901, Charles Richard John Spencer-Churchill, 9th Duke of Marlborough, sat down in his study overlooking the Italian Garden on the east side of Blenheim Palace, his magnificent honey-coloured Baroque home in Oxfordshire. Warmed by the blazing coal fire, he wrote of his failing marriage to Richard Burdon Haldane, a Liberal MP and lawyer. 'Sunny' Marlborough, as he was inappropriately nicknamed owing to his junior title, the Earl of Sunderland, had recently met this much-respected future Lord Chancellor at a weekend house party given by his aunt, Countess Howe.

Not unexpectedly, the 'arranged marriage' of five years earlier between this morose, irritable, highly-strung yet conscientious, sensitive and intelligent young aristocrat, to the beautiful American heiress Consuelo Vanderbilt was all but over. The possibility of a divorce meant scandal, public exposure and social ostracism. A distraught Sunny was in dire need of a heavyweight confidant:

Blenheim Palace.

My dear Mr Haldane,

I feel it is my duty after the kind manner in which you have aided me under circumstances which you have recognised to be extremely grave to give you a brief account of these domestic troubles which have occurred during the last few years, troubles which have created the present melancholy and difficult situation which, in order to overcome you have so generously

Lord Haldane seated on the right of Consuelo with Sunny standing left of his aunt, Lady Howe. 'Sunny was born to be small and slight of stature giving an appearance of weakness and fragility.'

proffered me not only your experience but also in the most thoughtful and delicate manner possible your personal assistance and advice.

In order that you may better understand the subsequent matters that I shall have to adhere to I will state that previous to my marriage in 1895 Consuelo had made the acquaintance of an American gentleman, Mr Rutherford [sic], for whom she entertained a regard and who she had wished to marry. In 1898 Mr Rutherford came to this country and stayed with us at Melton. A few weeks afterwards, Consuelo, together with Mrs Henry White, went to Paris and spent two weeks there while I was engaged in political work in England. I had some hesitation in allowing her to go but as Mrs White was her own countrywoman and a personal friend I felt that it would be ungenerous on my part to decline to allow her to go.

During the years 1898-1899 Mr Rutherford was a frequent visitor to this country. I did not like his companionship with Consuelo and I on several occasions stated to her that I did not approve of her friendship with him. At the same time I did not forbid her to see him at her own home in London as I had no just grounds for adopting that course. Mr Rutherford's visits occurred during the years 1898-1899 in London and also when Consuelo was in Paris. During the month of November in 1899 I had reason to make some strong comments to her with reference to her friendship with another gentleman which friendship I did not consider desirable.

This protest on my part led to a prolonged discussion with the result that Consuelo admitted to me that she had been on friendly terms and intimate relations with Mr Rutherford since the spring of 1898 when she met him in Paris. She stated moreover that she was devoted to him and that he was the one man to whom she had been attached in her life. She also told me that Mr Rutherford had frequently promised to elope with her in the event of her desiring to do so. I need hardly point out to you that I was placed in the most painful and trying position.

My first act was to write at once to Mrs Belmont, her mother, to come to England as I felt it was my duty to acquaint her of the situation and enlist her advice and help on her daughter's behalf. Mrs Belmont arrived in England on the 10th January 1900. Two weeks before this date Mr Rutherford came over from America on one of his visits to this country. He informed Consuelo of his arrival. She was anxious to go and see him and finally I allowed her to do so. Before she went however I pointed out to her in the plainest, yet at the same time kindest manner possible the exact position that she had placed herself in. I stated to her that I would not ask her to stay in my house if she desired to elope with Mr Rutherford but that in consideration of her youth, her inexperience and lack of knowledge of the world I would not force her away from her home and children. I told her that the decision must be made by her alone and pointed out to her with great care exactly what her position would be whatever course she adopted.

Consuelo went to London the day following this conversation. She had a long interview with Mr Rutherford and I gathered from her that he declined to elope with her on the plea that he was too attached to her. She told me she had no other course open to her but to remain with me and she displayed great sorrow and disgust at the base manner in which she had been deceived. She was conscious of the fact that she had ruined and wrecked the basis of her home life and that the prospect of the future was filled with sorrow. Mrs Belmont arrived from America a short time later and I acquainted her of the situation which she discussed with a lady relation of mine.

The call for Yeomanry Volunteers for the South African War was made by the government at this time and I decided to go with my regiment, the Queen's Own Oxfordshire Hussars. In the first place I decided it was my duty and in the second place I realised that it was my imperative that we should be separated for a few months. I felt moreover that in going to South Africa no one could detect any motive other than that which prompted everyone else who went and that I should enable Consuelo to live quietly for some months with her mother and to have an opportunity of recovering from the tragedy that had taken place.

I left for South Africa in January 1900 and I returned home at the end of July the same year. Within a short space of my arrival I gathered from Consuelo that she had become attached to someone during my absence. She moreover stated to me that a close intimacy between us was somewhat distasteful to her. These facts I communicated to the lady relation of whom I have had occasion to allude. In October 1900 I found that Consuelo was in friendly correspondence with my cousin Mr Frederick Guest who was in Egypt. I enquired the reason for this correspondence and she replied that she was fond of him and had seen him frequently in England during my absence abroad. In December I happened to return somewhat earlier than usual to my home in London and found Consuelo with another gentleman. They both received me in a confused manner.

A strong protest from me on her conduct led to a conversation in which she confessed to me that she had been on intimate relations with my cousin Mr Guest for a space of six weeks, that they had lived together in Paris while she was staying there with her father in a house on the river and also at my home, Blenheim. You will bear in mind that as soon as I heard these latter facts I felt it my duty to consult some legal opinion. I entrusted my confidence to you and you have been so kind and considerate as to interest yourself in the sad story. You will remember what my feelings were when I first came to see you.

You have asked me to follow your advice and great knowledge and experience. I shall make every endeavour to adhere to the course that you have after mature consideration laid down as the proper one to follow. You will believe that I find it most painful to have to record these terrible details of a story which is repugnant to me to have to allude to. I have written you a record of these events because I desire that my action throughout shall never be misinterpreted or misunderstood.

I have tried during the last eighteen months under circumstances and situations sometimes overwhelming in the sorrow and grief that they have brought me forcing me to bear the deepest feelings of misery, to sink entirely my own personal feelings and inclinations for these higher considerations which I felt that I was called upon to recognise.

That I should offer a young woman, the mother of my children, every equitable opportunity of repairing the error of the past and that I should strive, in spite of the shattered home to save her from herself from these terrible issues which her manner of life would inevitably lead her.

Believe me,

Yours sincerely,

Marlborough

From the evidence above Consuelo was almost certainly the first to break her marriage vows and not unnaturally, Sunny was always bitter about the fact. In retrospect, it is difficult to blame either side. Both these young people, who had the world at their feet, were in love with third parties and were pushed into marriage by their respective families in a deal of cash for coronets.

Consuelo was one of America's richest heiresses, being the great-granddaughter of 'the Commodore', Cornelius Vanderbilt, who built a vast fortune from shipping and railways. Her pushy and aggressive mother, Alva, whose ambitions for status and power were legendary,

Rutherfurd, seated second from the right, seen here in his polo kit. Consuelo's attachment to him was certainly sincere and lasting, even after she has 'forsaken all others' by marrying the Duke. Consuelo referred to Rutherfurd as her Rosenkavalier.

was desperate for Consuelo to marry an English Duke complete with his own palace.

When Sunny arrived in New York in the spring of 1895 he was described by the local press as 'the most eligible bachelor to arrive on our shores'. What they failed to recognise was that the Duke was nearly bankrupt. Four profligate dukes had dissipated the family fortune and in the process sold some of the finest pictures in the land together with the priceless Sunderland Library. On top of this tribal irresponsibility British agricultural income was steadily falling on the back of cheap imports from the Americas and Australasia and Sunny was forced to reduce the rents paid by his tenants.

Sunny's formidable grandmother, Fanny 7th Duchess of Marlborough, a daughter of the 3rd Marquess of Londonderry, had instilled in her grandson a strong sense of duty. He must forget the woman he loved and marry for money. From his earliest days it was bred into him that his life's purpose was to conserve and enrich Blenheim. In this endeavour he would eventually prove immensely successful but it would come at a dire cost to his own happiness.

Frances, known as Fanny, Duchess of Marlborough and her husband, the 7th Duke of Marlborough. She instilled in her grandson a strong sense of duty. He must forget the women he loved and marry for money.

1

Youth

Sunny Marlborough's character was an explosive cocktail of two opposites. On the one hand he was the model aristocrat, intelligent, learned, artistic, charming, graceful, urbane and patriotic with an inbuilt sense of duty, making him the perfect landlord and courtier. 'Fastidious and fussy- for at the bottom he was an aesthete, with a cult of perfection, whether in riding or in architecture, buildings, landscape, dress or women. In him the taste, the connoisseurship of his Spencer ancestors burned bright and clear.'[1] On the other hand, set against this buoyant exterior lay a darker side, a tortured, melancholic, irascible family man who could be reserved and awkward amongst outsiders. Sunny was in many ways the archetypical Edwardian duke. Proud, pompous and self-important, he was an enthusiastic upholder of the hierarchical society in which differences in rank were considered sacrosanct.

Sunny's complex personality points to an unhappy childhood and the observations of several close family members corroborate this theory. In her 1952 book *The Glitter and the Gold,* Consuelo complained that Sunny never exercised any discipline over their children because he had been bullied by his own father. His second wife, Gladys Deacon, confirmed his boyhood misery to her biographer, Hugo Vickers, stating: 'He was wounded as a child', whereas Anita Leslie in her book, *Jennie,* related how Sunny experienced: 'A crushed, unhappy boyhood.' Most revealingly, Sunny's favourite aunt, Maud, 5th Marchioness of Lansdowne, wrote to Gladys in December 1921:

The 8th Duke of Marlborough, Sunny's father. Highly intelligent and talented, but wayward and self indulgent.

Up to ten years old he was one of the most charming boys I have ever met and most joyous: after that his spirits seemed to have vanished and he quite changed but I have always remained very fond of him.

Charlie Londonderry wrote a telling letter to his and Sunny's cousin Winston Churchill in July 1934 congratulating him on the obituary he wrote on Sunny in *The Times*:

I am very sorry to hear of poor Sunny's death and send you all my affectionate sympathy because I know how fond you were of him and how proud he was of you and all your achievements. A hasty and ignorant judgement might condemn poor Sunny and you have informed many in obviously straightforward language the details of what must on the whole have been a sad life although at one time seemingly to hold out brilliant prospect. I think Sunny's childhood was badly mismanaged somehow: his pessimism always seemed to reflect an early grievance and I think he always imagined the world was against him.

It is almost certain that a specific, high profile public scandal, known generally as the 'Aylesford Affair' and as notorious perhaps as the Profumo crisis nearly a century later, was responsible for shattering his youthful spirit and leaving a permanent scar on his personality.

Sunny was born on 13 November 1871 in Simla, a Bengali hill station which was to become the summer capital of the British Raj. His parents, the Marquess and Marchioness of Blandford, were on a 'delayed honeymoon' visit to India where they enjoyed the hospitality of the Viceroy and his wife, Lord and Lady Mayo. Lord Blandford was an extremely clever, charming and entertaining individual but also an irresponsible, hell-raising womaniser who had been expelled from Eton and evicted from his regimental mess. Margaret Foster, biographer to the 7th Duchess of Marlborough described him as 'highly intelligent and talented but wayward and self-indulgent', the latter characteristics surely ensuring his eligibility for membership of the fashionable 'Marlborough House Set', a group of fast-living aristocrats surrounding the Prince of Wales who were renowned for their debauchery and marital infidelity. Marlborough House, originally built by the first Duke of Marlborough on land leased from Queen Anne had since reverted to the Crown and become the home of Bertie and Alexandra, the Prince and Princess of Wales. Sunny's grandparents were close friends and contemporaries of Queen Victoria so it was not unnatural for Blandford and his younger brother, Randolph Churchill to be readily accepted into the Prince's close circle.

In the early 1870's it was rumoured that the Prince of Wales was amicably sharing a mistress named Edith, Lady Aylesford, with his good friend Blandford. Edith was the well-connected wife of another member of the Marlborough House Set, the jolly, philandering, hard-drinking but not so bright 'Sporting Joe' Aylesford. According to Jane Ridley, the Prince's biographer, Queen Victoria was proven as canny as ever when she wrote to her private secretary:

It must be Edith whom Bertie admired rather than 'Sporting Joe' as Lord A. was too great a fool to be really agreeable to the P.O.W.

Edith came from a large family at the centre of London society whose wealth was based on copper mining in Wales. Her father, Thomas Peers-Williams was 'Father of the House of Commons' and M.P. for Marlow. Her brother, Owen Williams, was equerry to the Prince of Wales and one of her sisters was married to the Duke of Wellington.

In 1875 Bertie, accompanied by 'Sporting Joe', departed on a Grand Tour of India financed to the tune of over £200,000 by both Parliament and the Indian Government. The principal activity of the trip, much to the Queen's displeasure, was the unrestricted slaughter of tigers. The Prince's absence left the door to Packington Hall in Warwickshire, the Aylesford family estate, wide open and in walked Blandford who billeted himself at the local inn with his celebrated grey hunters. Blandford's passion for Edith soon became common knowledge in the local community and not unexpectedly, within a short period of time, news of their amorous exploits reached 'Sporting Joe' at his luxurious camp in the Indian bush.

On 20 February 1876 'Sporting Joe' received a letter from Edith asking for a divorce. She confessed she was in love with Blandford who intended to elope with her and divorce his own long-suffering wife Albertha, daughter of the Duke of Abercorn and sister-in-law to the Marquess of Lansdowne. Not unnaturally, an irate 'Sporting Joe' immediately left for England, threatening both a duel with Blandford and a divorce action against his wife. The reckless threesome had at one stroke placed a powder keg under the Marlborough House Set and the upper echelons of stuffy, hypocritical, Victorian society. Infidelity was accepted as long as it was not discovered. Divorce, on the other hand was taboo, as it brought public exposure in the courts and social disgrace on all concerned.

Sunny with his mother Albertha, daughter of the Duke of Abercorn.

What made the Aylesford affair so infamous was the involvement of the heir to the throne. If the rakish lifestyle of the Marlborough House Set was publicly exposed, the country could face a constitutional crisis. Bertie had already been involved in the Mordaunt divorce case of 1870 and the careers of two famous public figures, Charles Parnell and Oscar Wilde, had both been destroyed by their immorality being made public. Blandford's brilliant yet impetuous brother, Randolph, was determined to prevent a divorce which would disgrace the family name. His outlandish solution was to blackmail the Prince of Wales. Edith had stupidly provided her lover with some letters 'of a compromising nature' written to her by the Prince which Blandford immediately passed on to his brother. Randolph, demonstrating remarkable cheek and insensitivity, decided to call on Princess Alexandra, the Princess of Wales, and reveal the presence of the letters.

He hoped she would persuade Bertie to stop 'Sporting Joe' from pressing ahead with his divorce. Much to the Duke and Duchess of Marlborough's horror the Queen was dragged in to the embarrassing business. Standing firmly by her son and claiming the 'innocence' of the letters she advised him not to get involved. Total disgrace was averted by 'Sporting Joe' who 'in order to avoid great public mischief' decided against divorce in favour of a private legal separation.

The fallout from the scandal reached far and wide. Randolph gave the Prince a half-hearted apology who in turn stated he would not visit any house that entertained the Spencer-Churchills. Rather than become a social outcast as a result of his son's behaviour, the Duke of Marlborough accepted Benjamin Disraeli, the Prime Minister's, offer to become Viceroy of Ireland in 1877. Although he did not know it then, this would have fatal consequences for many of the family heirlooms at Blenheim which would need to be sold to repay debts incurred by the Duke whilst serving as the Queen's representative. The salary was £20,000 a year and the realistic costs of running Dublin Castle were over £40,000. Randolph and his new American wife Jennie accompanied the Duke. Working as private secretary to his father proved the launch pad for Randolph's meteoric political career.

'Sporting Joe' disappeared to America where he bought 20,000 acres in Texas and died of alcoholism at the age of thirty-six. The two central figures in the scandal, Edith and Lord Blandford, fled to Paris and lived happily for a few years at the Hotel Rivoli under the name of Spencer.

Lord Randolph Churchill,
Sunny's brilliant uncle.

Blandford's wife, Albertha, meanwhile kept her head down at their country house, Oakdene, near Dorking. She was not an overly intelligent woman and had a tiresome penchant for practical jokes which drove her husband to distraction but she had spirit and a mind of her own. Her relationship with Blandford had completely broken down by the summer of 1875.

In March 1878 she finally obtained a deed of separation which ensured she received maintenance and secured the right to live at Oakdene. She was also granted custody of their four children including Sunny who was six years old at the time. One can only imagine that aside from missing his father, being so young and locked away in the country, Sunny weathered the worst aspects of the Aylesford storm reasonably well. But this was a scandal that was going to run and run.

In the summer of 1878 'Sporting Joe' brought a divorce case against his wife and Blandford was a co-respondent. On 4 July the divorce was

*Sunny's grandfather
and his family at
Blenheim below the steps
overlooking the garden on
the east side of the Palace.*

disallowed on grounds of collusion and shortly afterwards the Bland-
fords attempted to patch up their marriage. Oakdene was sold and they
rented a house in Cadogan Square living together until April 1882 when
Albertha discovered her husband had sired an illegitimate son, Guy Bertrand. These years must have placed an enormous emotional strain on
Sunny and laid the foundations for his complex personality developed in
later life.

In 1883, after years of public humiliation at the hands of the adul-
terous Blandford, Albertha secured a divorce on grounds of his adultery,
desertion and cruelty. She was given custody of their three daughters
however the 7th Duke secured part legal guardianship of his grandson.
Understandably the Duke was determined that Sunny should learn all
about his future duties and responsibilities at Blenheim. *The Times* commented: 'It was considered essential for the welfare of the boy that he
should be brought up in connection with the great estate which he was

to inherit', and that he, 'have the opportunity of becoming acquainted with the large body of people who at a future time would be his own tenantry.' Thus Sunny became separated from his mother and sisters.

To complicate matters further the 7th Duke died soon after this arrangement was made and Duchess Fanny petitioned to assume her husband's role. She was supported by two male trustees, the Duke of Abercorn and Edward Marjoribanks who were both Sunny's uncles. They later instigated legal proceedings on behalf of Sunny regarding the 8th Duke's mismanagement of the Blenheim Estate. This drove a further wedge between father and son.

In 1883, Sunny suffered further humiliation when 'Sporting Joe' Aylesford's younger brother had a male heir and Edith decided to bring her son with Blandford, named Guy Bertrand, back from Paris and baptize him at St Mary-le-Strand. The whole of London society now knew of Blandford's illegitimate son who was optimistically titled Lord Guernsey, as if he were the son and heir of the Earl of Aylesford. In 1885 'Sporting Joe' died in America and the Dowager Lady Aylesford and her younger son disputed the paternity of Lord Guernsey. So began the time-honoured Aylesford Peerage Case which concluded with the House of Lords disallowing Edith's paternity claim. Sunny's father, by then the 8th Duke of Marlborough, was called to give evidence at the hearing and shortly afterwards parted from a distraught Edith. It was rumoured he pleaded with Edith to bring up Guy, whom he said he loved better than any of his four children. In the event Guy spent a good deal of time at Blenheim from 1885 until 1892 which must have been most uncomfortable for Sunny.

By the age of fourteen, Sunny had spent his childhood in a 'broken home', been up-rooted from Oakdene, experienced his parent's divorce, seen little of his father, been separated from his mother and sisters, and perhaps, for a proud child, worst of all, witnessed the Spencer-Churchill name being 'blackened' publically in the courts and national press.

To make matters worse, his grandfather was selling off the family heirlooms at Blenheim. The family finances had been in a precarious state for some years but the 7th Duke's tenure in Ireland had exacerbated the problem. In 1875 he had sold off not only the 4th Duke's Gem collection but also the Waddesdon Estate to Ferdinand de Rothschild. This was followed in the summer of 1882 by the sale of the fabulous

Sunny as a Prefect at Winchester where he developed two of his abiding interests – a love of cricket and a fascination for politics.

Sunderland Library. In 1885 Sunny's father continued this trend and set about Blenheim's priceless picture collection, of which nine masterpieces went abroad. To put things into perspective, when the 8th Duke died prematurely at the age of forty-eight, he left his mistress, Lady Colin Campbell, £20,000 in his will, having sold the Equestrian Van Dyk of Charles 1st for £17,500 a few years previously. It is no surprise that Sunny developed into such a complicated and highly-strung individual.

In January 1884 Sunny was sent to board at Winchester College. Little is known of his prior education except that he had attended Dr Girdlestone's school, in Ascot. A childhood spell in the Palace schoolroom with a private tutor also seems likely. One must assume the young teenager was teased mercilessly in those early days as the drawn-out family saga ran its tragic course, merely thirty years after the publication of *Tom Brown's Schooldays*.

It is interesting to note that Sunny attended Winchester, as the Spencer-Churchill family had gone to Eton for generations. Although Sunny's paternal grandfather, the 7th Duke, assumed the responsibility of paying for his education, it has been suggested that Winchester was chosen because it was one of the few schools with a science faculty. The 8th Duke was a brilliant scientist who installed his own laboratory at Blenheim. Sunny spent five years in J.T. Bramston's House (Culvers Close) where he developed two of his abiding interests, a love of cricket and a fascination for politics. He played cricket for his house and in his last year joined the school debating society.

On 4 October 1890 Sunny went up to Trinity College, Cambridge to read history. He shared lodgings at 7 Bridge Street with his cousin, Ivor Guest, later Viscount Wimborne, but did not graduate at the end of his three years. In late Victorian times many members of the aristocracy went up to Cambridge but did not graduate as it was a means of 'preparing themselves for society and making useful contacts.' On 11 November 1892, a few days after the death of his father, the *New York Times* ran an article on the recently elevated, undergraduate Duke, stating that he was: 'an able student, a clever polo and cricket player and a bold rider to hounds.' Sunny was a fine horsemen and became Master of the Cambridge University Draghounds. He continued to develop an interest in politics by joining Trinity's debating society, the *Magpie and Stump*, at the time when Erskine Childers was President. The latter lodged at 5 Bridge Street and became celebrated with the publication of his book, *The Riddle of the Sands*. At Cambridge, Childers was close to intellectuals such as Eddie Marsh, Winston Churchill's Private Secretary, and Walter Runcimann. Sunny played his part in the University's social life by joining the elite Athenaeum and Pitt Clubs which tended to be frequented by the more sports orientated undergraduates.

Unsurprisingly the *New York Times* was more critical of Sunny's undergraduate career following his engagement to Consuelo. On 27 October 1895 it stated:

Sunny excited no personal enthusiasm at Cambridge or elsewhere' and 'in all that it said of him you get an effect of scrupulous decorum, a trifle chilly and priggish if anything.

In Sunny's defence, the local press at this time was pregnant with unpleasant stories regarding English aristocrats absconding with American

Sunny standing third from the left in the picture as a member of the Cambridge Athenaeum Club.

'dollar princesses'. The University newspaper, *Granta*, was more gratuitous, writing on his twenty-first birthday:

> He came to Cambridge two years ago, a small and neat little fellow; but he soon showed that he had reached his proper sphere and began by flooring the boldest examiners whom Trinity could boast.

Granta pointed to his appreciation of art and developing sense of taste that would prove such a strength in years to come:

> He has great tastes in colours and his rooms present a pleasing mixture of reds and greens. He is well known to the Bond Street dealers in the antique who declare that he is quite incapable of bad taste.

After he left Cambridge in 1893 the eligible young Duke divided his time between Blenheim and London. He developed close relationships with several society debutantes, one of which it was rumoured he was

Sunny dressed as a member of the Cambridge University 'True Blue' dining club.

deeply in love with and wished to marry. The other was desperate to capture him.

Lady Angela St Clair Erskine was the youngest daughter of the 4th Earl of Rosslyn. In 1895 when she became close to Sunny, she was nineteen years old, nearly six feet tall, vivacious, full of life, with a passion for hunting and, it was said, 'the vocabulary of a stable boy.' There is little doubt she had ambitions of her own as her four elder sisters had all married extremely well. Of her two full sisters, one married the Duke of Sutherland and the other the Earl of Westmorland, while her half-sisters were to prove just as successful in their endeavours. Daisy became the wife of the Earl of Warwick in addition to becoming the favourite mistress of the Prince of Wales, while Blanche married Lord Algernon Gordon-Lennox. It was no secret she was making a play for Sunny. Winston writing to his mother from Blenheim in 1895 recorded:

> I rode in the park chiefly with Lady Angela – who is not bad company – I think she is trying all she knows to capture Sunny.

Angela was a famously brave foxhunter in the shires. Born with an attractive self-confidence and a wicked sense of humour she no doubt struck an immediate chord with the dashing young Duke, himself an accomplished horseman. Apparently, after she had lost Sunny to Consuelo and when proposed to by her future husband Lt-Colonel James Forbes she answered: 'Yes, if I can have your chestnut mare.'

Sunny's whirlwind romance with Angela probably began in Melton around Christmas 1895 while hunting with the Quorn in Leicestershire. It continued throughout the spring and summer until in August he left for America to marry Consuelo. There are a series of letters at Blenheim over this period from Angela to Sunny demonstrating a developing friendship as she addresses him as firstly 'My dear Duke', then 'My dear Sunny' and finally as he leaves for New York in August 1895 as 'Sunny darling'. The affair was almost certainly one-sided as Sunny was still in love with a former girlfriend. On 15 June Alva took Consuelo down to Blenheim for the first time, the central part of her plot to marry her daughter off to one of England's foremost aristocrats. In her book *Consuelo and Alva*, Amanda Mackenzie Stuart writes:

> That very afternoon Sunny would set aside his feelings for an English girl with whom he was in love and marry Consuelo.

There is no reference to who 'the English girl' was but it is unlikely to have been Angela.

Events moved on quickly after that fateful weekend. Sunny decided to put family duty before his personal happiness and Alva's Machiavellian designs consigned Consuelo to years of misery. Angela ironically appears in the Blenheim Visitors Book the following weekend. Her thank-you letter from Bishops Farm, Windsor, proves both her anger at her betrayal and the depth of their relationship:

> By the by knowing me as well as you do why didn't you tell me you had settled that little affair with Mrs Vanderbilt before they left; also that the trip abroad is for business as well as pleasure. Well, I hope you will be happy and if not, it will be your own fault.

Alva, of course, wasted no time in executing her plans. Sunny embarked for America on 16 August the engagement was announced on 20 September and the unhappy couple were married in a blaze of publicity on

Sunny circa 1894 the dashing man about town. Having left Cambridge he developed close relations with several society women. One of whom, it was rumoured he was deeply in love with and wished to marry. The other was desperate to capture him.

6 November at St Thomas Church, New York. A short time before the wedding Angela was writing to Sunny from Easton, her sister Daisy's family home in Essex:

> It is horrible to feel that in a few weeks I shall have no right to scribble my thoughts to you. Ever since I came out you have been mysteriously connected with all my good times and I cannot bear to feel that they are all over, for you are right, those really happy moments except in a few exceptional cases never occur again.

The following year Angela wrote to Sunny informing him that she was to follow the ducal example and marry for convenience. The bridegroom was their mutual Melton hunting friend, Lt-Colonel James Forbes who

The eligible young Duke, an accomplished horseman, at the time of his romance with Angela St Clare Erskine, in the New Year 1896.

appeared in the Blenheim Visitors Book in 1894. She pathetically told Sunny on her wedding day, 27 April 1896:

> Jim is the person who deserves most sympathy as I know how badly I have often behaved to him and now that the day has come I realise how much fairer it would have been to him to have told him at once I did not care but having said 'yes' I stuck to it thinking it was for his happiness and that I should grow fonder. Today is the most miserable day of my life. Bless you again for your letter and do not forget.

Sunny and Angela remained good friends and she stayed at Blenheim on 7 August 1896 but there are no further entries in the Visitors Book.

It was just as well that Sunny never considered marriage to Angela.

Aside from the fact she had little money she was an unpredictable maverick. She lived her life 'on the edge', scandal was never far from her side and with an abrasive manner, together with a complete disregard for red tape she made many enemies. By 1912 she was the acknowledged mistress of Lord Elcho, later the 9th Earl of Wemyss, with whom she shared a passion for gambling. These two aristocrats were as 'thick as thieves', travelled widely together, and were involved in an embarrassing and public court case concerning Wemyss family paintings. Angela had been selling a number of her lover's paintings on commission without his prior permission and legal proceedings were commenced by an intermediary who failed to receive the works of art. Amongst her other lovers was Lord Ribblesdale, immortalised in his hunt coat by society painter, John Singer Sargent. Edith Sitwell wrote cruelly of Angela in later life:

> She was a bad hangover from the Edwardian era. This household pest strongly resembled in colour, figure and profile and in general, the impression of tattered hairiness, an elderly gorilla afflicted with sex appeal.

Before Angela's brief, unrequited affair with Sunny it was rumoured he was engaged to Muriel Wilson, the beautiful, youngest daughter of Arthur Wilson of Hull, considered at the turn of the twentieth century to be the wealthiest ship owner in the world. Muriel had much in common with Angela. Both girls were dashing horsewomen and intelligent extroverts. They were considered to be two of the most eccentric girls in high society, Muriel being a talented amateur actress with a most nonconformist dress sense. Sunny was not surprisingly attracted to such exquisite, energetic and unconventional female company which provided a welcome contrast to his experiences with the opposite sex during a drab, unhappy, Victorian childhood. Muriel was the love of Sunny's life but tragically for his personal happiness they never married.

Muriel's fragrant persona, however, was tainted by a whiff of scandal. In early September 1890 the Prince of Wales was staying with Muriel's father for a partridge shoot at his country estate, Tranby Croft. One evening members of the house party were playing baccarat, an illegal gambling card game that was a favourite pastime of the Prince when one of the guests, Sir William Gordon-Cumming, was caught cheating. The culprit agreed to sign a pledge that he would never play cards again in

Sunny as Master of the Cambridge University Draghounds 1892. His first cousin and close friend, Ivor Guest, is on the right of the picture.

exchange for an agreement that his misdemeanours would be kept secret. Needless to say word reached the press, probably through the indiscretions of the Prince's mistress, Angela's sister, Daisy Brooke, also known as the 'Babbling Brook'. Sir William decided to defend his reputation in court and much to the embarrassment of the Establishment the Prince was compelled to testify. With the humiliation of the Mordaunt adultery case of 1870 still fresh, the heir to the throne found himself once again disgraced by scandal. The repercussions were felt far and wide. The jury found against Sir William. He was dismissed from the army, the Prince dropped his mistress, Daisy Brooke, which presented a vacancy for Mrs Keppel, and the Wilsons quietly withdrew from society in much the same way as Sunny's grandfather had done a generation earlier over the Aylesford affair.

On 1 March 1894 Sunny received a letter from his cousin Ivor Guest who was in India. Ivor was the son of the 1st Baron Wimborne whose fortune was made from the Dowlais ironworks in South Wales. Wimborne's wife, Lady Cornelia Spencer-Churchill, was Sunny's aunt. Sunny and Ivor and in addition, Winston Churchill, all became life-long friends proving that relations among first cousins can be as close as that between brothers but without any of the sibling rivalry. A letter written by Alice Wimborne on Ivor's death in June 1939 proves how close the three cousins were:

> In his heart there was Winston and Sunny and no one else he knew or liked in any way competed with these two who were far more to him than any of his brothers or indeed anyone else on earth except little Ivor and myself. He was never the same after Sunny went.

So close were the cousins that Sunny christened his second son, Ivor.

In Ivor's letter he addressed Sunny as 'My dear old friend', and continued, 'I don't know why I have begun in this unconventional way except that it expresses what I feel.'

He was emphatic that Sunny should not marry Muriel. He admitted that she was 'a fascinating and attractive girl' and encouraged him to take an overseas trip 'to take your thoughts from other things'. Ivor not only reminded Sunny of the scandal attached to the Wilson family but also made the point that his cousin was too young to be tied down by children which in turn would necessitate foregoing the opportunity of foreign travel. Most interestingly he wrote, 'you can't afford it and you must marry some money'. By 'some money' he obviously meant considerable amounts of money as Muriel was not poor. He continued:

> A year or two at Blenheim should soon convince you that with her and your expensive tastes that you could live there no longer in any of the decent splendour in which you live', and amusingly, 'and it would be your mother-in-law and all her family who would certainly make the most of a ducal relation and cause you trouble.

Ivor was worried that Blenheim was becoming a millstone around its proprietor's neck and was inhibiting any ambitions Sunny had in other directions, such as politics. He added:

> Perhaps are you in love because you are living at Blenheim and bored with life? You seem to be in a cul-de-sac and you grasp eagerly at any ray of light which shines through the dull wall which blocks your immediate

prospect of advance. We cannot live without an object and that is what you want and consequently, naturally turn to love as holding out some pleasing prospect for the future and happiness in the present.

So it was not just Sunny's venerable old grandmother, Fanny Marlborough who wished him to marry for money. There was pressure from young and old alike who wanted to see Blenheim restored to its former glory. In all likelihood there was a hint of jealousy behind Ivor's advice as in the same letter he admitted to having been in love with Muriel. In fact, she cast her spell over all three Churchill cousins as Winston proposed to her early in 1904 and was rejected. Mary Lovell, in *The Churchills*, recalls how in love Winston was when he wrote to Muriel:

> Don't slam the door...I can wait – perhaps I shall improve with waiting. Why shouldn't you care about me some day? I have great faith in my instinct...Time and circumstance will work for me...I love you because you are good and beautiful.

Ironically, unlike the Prime Minister's daughter, Violet Asquith, who was fascinated by Winston when meeting him a few years later and instantly recognised his genius, Muriel felt that Winston was not good enough for her and had no prospects.

Ivor certainly had Sunny's best interests at heart. He appreciated how seriously his cousin was now taking his ducal obligations and how his duty to Blenheim as a life tenant was of paramount personal importance. He wrote on 8 September by which time he had dropped the idea of marrying Muriel:

> You have changed much since Cambridge and I admire you greatly for having been willing to sacrifice worldly selfishness for an unselfish affection and that your sense of duty finally controlled you; Noblesse oblige, and the greater the position, the greater the obligation. Much is demanded of you; to some extent the greatest of all things, the sacrifice of one's personal sympathies. You are lonely at Blenheim and life is sometimes bleak. I sincerely hope that you may be granted a wife whom you will grow to love, honour and respect more and more as the years roll by and who will also prove a material help to you in your duties in life.

Sunny a serious young man on his way to New York to become engaged to one of the richest heiresses in the world.

Ivor was concerned he was too forward in his previous letter of 1 March and backtracked on his advice to marry for money:

> I wish you would disassociate from yourself the idea of 'selling yourself'. Don't marry for money but go where money is in moderation.

As it turned out, of course, Sunny stuck to his cousin's original advice and by marrying Consuelo captured the richest heiress in the world. At the same time Ivor was well aware of Sunny's weakness for the good life and his requirement for additional cash resources for he wrote in the same letter:

> I tried to appeal to the heart through the head. I appeal to the worldly side not because I particularly care for money but because I think you have expensive tastes and one saddled with a great possession, the which,

if you have not the means to maintain as you would like and would become an incumbent on you.

Ivor knew his cousin all too well. Sunny would demand to live at Blenheim in the grand style that his ducal ancestors had for generations. Sure enough, Sunny kept up his standards, even after the First World War. According to Duff Cooper, a Conservative politician and socialite, writing in his diary on 16 June 1920:

> I have never seen Blenheim before and was much impressed by its beauty and magnificence. The Duke keeps high state. Wears his Garter for dinner and has a host of powdered footman.

There seems little doubt that on leaving Cambridge Sunny decided to put his duty to Blenheim first and marry for money. He was certainly being offered advice from all quarters of the family to do so, including well known public figures such as his uncles, Randolph Churchill and Lord Lansdowne. In a perfect world it was generally agreed that Sunny, even if not in love, at the very least should like and respect his future bride. Lansdowne wrote to Sunny from his home, Derreen, in Ireland on 22 September 1895 to congratulate him on his engagement to Consuelo:

> I believe you have made a wise choice. I would not for the world have you marry for money alone but it was essential that your wife should contribute something to the 'menage' and the problem was to find one who should do this and also be attractive and likely to be a successful mistress of the house at Blenheim as well as make you happy in your home.

He continued:

> Nor do I believe, my dear Sunny in spite of some rather cynical remarks that you made for your old uncle's clarification that you would have asked her to marry you if you had not made up your mind that you would be really fond of her and also to make her happy as well as yourself.

However it appears from correspondence with his Uncle Randolph in August 1894 that Sunny was willing to take a shockingly cynical

The 5th Marquess of Lansdowne, Sunny's uncle and close confident.

approach to acquiring a prospective heiress. Randolph was on a world tour to America and Japan in the year before he died. He wrote to Sunny:

> I have told you a good deal about my proceedings and I now wish to notice some of the interesting remarks and arguments which you have written me in your letter of the 6th just. I agree with you about Miss Vanderbilt. She is a Jewess. Then you say, 'I don't think I could marry anyone I did not like unless I got a good equivalent in return, say one million'. Well I think by narrowing such a sum as that you put a bar on marrying for money. There are few millions in England which I know of at the present moment and which would accord with your stipulation of personal liking.

Randolph obviously believed Sunny was making the correct decision in prospecting across the Atlantic as there were few obvious candidates on

Muriel Wilson by John Singer Sargent. The love of Sunny's life?

home soil. In referring to his future wife as 'a Jewess' when there was little or no Jewish blood in the Vanderbilt family and with Consuelo well capable of producing a dowry in excess of 'one million' one might well be forgiven for deducing that the Sunny was not on the best of terms with his future bride when Alva Vanderbilt forced her daughter into marriage.

The strain of maintaining the Palace together with his two failed marriages would come at a terrible cost to Sunny's happiness. Tellingly, nowadays, Sargent's charcoal drawing of Muriel Wilson sits just below his portrait of Sunny in a passage off the Great Hall at Blenheim. She was distraught at Sunny's death and not feeling strong enough to go to his funeral wrote to Winston:

> Your appreciation of Sunny was so wonderful – it said exactly all that his friends loved in him and I am quite sure that now he has gone many will realise what a charming and delightful character he had.

The lesson to be learned is that the pursuit of money and status leads only to unhappiness and a failed marriage. Consuelo should have been allowed to wed Winthrop Rutherfurd by her overbearing mother and Gladys Deacon, Sunny's second wife, should have married the cultured Italian aristocrat, Roffredo Caetani. Both wives were independent characters complete with strong personalities. Sunny failed dismally to cope with them on an emotional level. They denied him the affection he was incapable of seeking. Sunny who was reserved and buttoned-up, needed a woman who would envelope him with the love he so sorely missed in his childhood. Perhaps Muriel Wilson was that very person. She ended her letter to Winston with these despairing words:

> I am quite sure Sunny is the happiest, to have escaped all the tiresome messes of this life and it is only we who are left to miss him who are the unlucky ones.

2

The 9th Duke's engagement,
wedding and first year
of married life

The engagement

Sunny and Consuelo were married at St. Thomas' Church, which stood at the corner of 5th Avenue and 53rd Street, in New York on 6 November 1895. The wedding had been eagerly anticipated by Consuelo's mother Alva, by the Duke's family and by the American Press. The only people who were not eagerly looking forward to the day were bride and groom. Neither loved the other and sadly, after their marriage, they did not learn to love each other. Consuelo had been instructed to marry Sunny by her mother. He had been instructed, by his grandmother to find a wealthy bride whose funds would rescue Blenheim and who would produce an heir.

The *New York Recorder* believed it was Lilian Hammersley, the second wife of the 8th Duke and an American, who introduced Consuelo to the 9th Duke with the intention that they should marry. Lilian may have had a hand in proceedings but it was Alva who was the driving force.

Before Consuelo met Sunny she was in love with an American called Winthrop Rutherfurd. He was by the standards of the time a perfectly respectable match for Consuelo. He came from a New England family who numbered amongst their ancestors a former Colonial Governor of New York, Peter Stuyvesant and John Winthrop, the first Governor of Massachusetts. They were well off and moved in the same social circles as the elite of Newport. As far as Alva was concerned, however, Winthrop was not an acceptable match. She had designs on a European husband and in particular a European husband with a title. Winthrop

A painting of Consuelo by Carolus Duran. Consuelo said that this painting had been commissioned so that she could take her place amongst the other beauties displayed on Blenheim's walls. In reality it was commissioned by Alva in 1894, to hang in Marble House in the hope of attracting the right groom. After the wedding it was moved to Blenheim where it hangs in the First State Room.

Rutherfurd proposed, in secret, to Consuelo on 2 March 1895. Shortly after this Alva and Consuelo went to Europe, first to France and then to England.

In France Alva purchased the best of haute couture for her daughter and in London she ensured Consuelo was introduced to all the right people. During the London season Consuelo and her mother were invited to a ball given by the Duke and Duchess of Sutherland and Sunny claimed several dances from Consuelo. To Alva's delight he then issued an invitation to visit Blenheim.

Consuelo and Alva travelled to Blenheim on 15 June 1895 to stay for the weekend. Others in the party were Minnie Paget and two of Sunny's sisters, Lady Lilian and Lady Norah. The Duke showed Consuelo the

*A view of Blenheim Palace taken across the Lake. This is the view
Consuelo and her mother saw when they came through the Woodstock
Gate into the Park in June 1895.*

Park and part of the nearby estate. He was charming and Consuelo herself said she was enchanted by the countryside and the deference shown
to him by all the local people. She did not, however, wish to marry him.
Alva immediately engineered the next step and invited him to come to
her Summer Ball in August in Newport. He accepted the invitation and
travelled to America on the steamer 'Campania', which left Liverpool
on 16 August 1895. He arrived in New York on 23 August and the
press were waiting for him. He did his best to avoid the barrage of
questions but one journalist finally managed to corner him in his hotel
and bluntly asked him about his plans. He courteously replied that he
intended to explore America 'west and south'. He also planned to go to
Hawaii, Australia, Japan, China and the Indies. Of course he only got
as far as Newport.

The newspapers gave detailed descriptions of the Duke both in terms
of his physical appearance and the clothes he wore. It would seem that

Sunny pausing during a game of tennis with Lady Birkenhead at Lord and Lady Birkenhead's house in Charlton, a village not far from the Palace.

their readers could not get enough information about this English aristocrat. Sometimes the newspapers were kind and described him in the most pleasant of terms:

The Duke is slight, but well built, … has light brown hair, and a slight brownish moustache. His eyes are blue and their expression is of the utmost frankness and kindliness, and as his face lights up with merriment, as it constantly does in conversation, the eyes twinkle.

This description does not quite fit the very serious young man most people knew Sunny to be and perhaps the *Herald* of Boston got closer to the truth when stating that: 'The Duke of Marlborough appears to be a nice sort of chap.' That newspaper went on to say that he seemed surprised by all the attention he was receiving from journalists. Alva, Consuelo's mother, was however very pleased with the column inches given to her future son-in-law.

Sunny stayed at the Waldorf Hotel and made a tour of the city in an open carriage with an acquaintance of his, Creighton Webb. They had lunch at Delmonico's on 5th Avenue and the next day he travelled to Newport by train.

Newport society was agog and his every move was closely watched. Everything he did was reported in full detail. On 30 August a large crowd gathered to watch a tennis match between him and Tom Pettit, 'the champion of the world'. As it turned out it was not a tennis match but a tennis lesson. The newspaper rather unkindly commented: 'The Duke picked up a racquet rather clumsily and the spectators were surprised to

Marble House in Newport, Rhode Island. The house is now open to the public and is cared for by the Preservation Society of Newport County.

see Mr Pettit begin to show him how to hold it.' The lesson went on for three-quarters of an hour with Mr Pettit keeping him running round the court. The newspaper finished by saying: 'The Duke will take a lesson every day he is here and when he returns abroad he will understand something of the game.' Undoubtedly Sunny would have preferred to learn the game without being in full view of the crowd.

In Newport he was plunged into a social whirl. Alva ensured that as far as possible he escorted Consuelo and that in turn the young couple were chaperoned by her and her alone. Sunny attended the ball given on 26 August by Richard T. Wilson at the Golf Club. He also attended a dance at the Casino and a ball at Marble House which was a deliberately lavish and excessive affair. Alva left no stone unturned to impress her guests. The next day Sunny had dinner at Marble House, naturally seated next to Consuelo. The food was delicious, the flowers overwhelming, the music sublime, the guests plentiful and all of them excited at the prospect of Consuelo becoming a Duchess. The social engagements and invitations poured in. Sunny, Consuelo and Alva were entertained on the yacht of John Jacob Astor. They had leisurely drives to the Casino to meet with Newport's elite. There were luncheons and dinners where the champagne flowed.

It was at Marble House, Consuelo's home, where, as Consuelo wrote many years later: 'In the comparative quiet of an evening at home Marlborough proposed in the Gothic Room.' Triumphant, the next day Sunny departed to explore a little more of America, a country he told Consuelo that he had no intention of ever visiting again.

Alva was jubilant and the engagement was formally announced on 20 September. She saw no reason for a lengthy engagement and initially fixed the date of the wedding for 5 November. Not wanting to get married on the anniversary of the day Guy Fawkes attempted to blow up Parliament, Sunny requested the day after. They were married on 6 November, any sooner and it would have been impossible for even a woman like Alva to arrange the wedding with due magnificence.

The wedding

The American newspapers were out in force to report on the wedding of the year. The *New York Recorder* ran with the following headlines:

Consuelo is Duchess of Marlborough
Wedded to the young Duke with gorgeous ceremony
Immense crowd at scene
Two hundred policemen kept busy in preserving order
Magnificent costumes, rare decorations and a brilliant assemblage of
New York's Social notables helped to make the Nuptials impressive

The weather on the day started foggy but the sun broke through. The whole event went perfectly from start to finish as far as the bride's mother was concerned. From Sunny's point of view there were a few worrying moments. As his carriage drew up at the church it was surrounded by a huge crowd of women, all of whom surged forward in an attempt to not only see him but also touch him. The *New York Recorder* commented that as he tried to walk to the church the women nearest: 'Petted him. … The Duke got into the church after his clothes and hat were ruffled.' He entered through the side door of the church, somewhat red in the face.

Consuelo and her father William K. Vanderbilt, on a happier occasion.

Then there followed a commotion near the 5th Avenue entrance. A policeman came out dragging with him a young newspaper boy, Jerry McQuillan, who was in tears. The newspaper reported that:

Jerry had been discovered by an Usher sitting in one of the reserved seats in the middle aisle near the centre of the Church, deeply engrossed in the brilliant costumes and huge banks of flowers. He had been in the pew several minutes before he was discovered.[1]

The newspapers gave a detailed analysis of every aspect of the wedding, describing the wedding gifts, how the guests were attired, the floral displays in the church, the hymns, the music, the bridesmaids and the best man.

The newspapers said that the best man, Ivor Guest, 'chatted with the Duke smilingly' and seemed oblivious to all that was going on around him. Sunny, however, was reported to have been very nervous, every now and then looking to the door of the church through which Consuelo would enter. His nerves were not calmed when it became clear that Consuelo was going to be late. She was in fact twenty minutes late and by then the congregation were also beginning to feel uneasy. When the carriage finally arrived carrying the bride and her father, the crowd surged forward and the police had a very difficult time keeping order. The *New York Recorder* noted:

Mr Vanderbilt stepped from the carriage first, and carried in both hands the great Blenheim bridal bouquet fashioned after the model which has been used in the Marlborough family for centuries…The bouquet was so large that very little of Mr. Vanderbilt could be seen…A maid stepped forward to assist Consuelo from her carriage. She was radiant in her lovely gown…The maids arranged the point lace veil and coronet of orange blossoms.

Mr Vanderbilt appeared to be in sombre mood and outwardly at least did not seem to be overjoyed that his daughter was marrying into the English aristocracy. The same newspaper noted that:

> He was the only one of the Vanderbilt family whose face was not wreathed in smiles. He looked very solemn, indeed, in his black clothes and high hat, and if he had been going to a funeral his expression could not have been more gloomy.

Of course the newspapers spent a great deal of time describing the bride's dress and the clothes worn by the groom. According to one American newspaper he wore, 'A grey frock coat which fitted his figure snugly.' Another newspaper went into more detail and suggested that he had been somewhat modern in the way he dressed:

> The Duke wore a suit of grey cloth, a long frock coat and trousers of the same material, and a large boutonniere. A grey suit for a wedding is rather an innovation in New York, and the fact that the Duke so attired himself produced much comment. Mr. Guest wore a conventional black diagonal suit, with frock coat, and also introduced the novelty at even a morning wedding of a light blue shirt, of course with a white collar.

Consuelo's dress was a triumph:

> It was of satin of a creamy tint, and matching the rare point lace with which it was trimmed. The lace covered the entire front of both skirt and bodice. Upon the former it was arranged in four horizontal, 12-inch deep rows, reaching clear across the front and sides and hiding the satin underneath. Upon the right side and crossing the flounces diagonally was a long spray of orange blossoms. Underneath the lowest flounce upon the skirt edge was a narrow spray of orange blossoms. The front of the corsage was draped with chiffon gathered very full from the neck to belt, and over this fell a deep frill of lace. The high collar was covered in lace,

and at the waist the bodice was finished with a satin girdle. The sleeves were very large, being pleated into the armhole and fitting gauntlet style below the elbow, without trimming of any sort.

Upon the left shoulder was a spray of orange blossoms, and over each sleeve projected triple revers of lace. The pattern of the lace appeared to be the combination known as point d'Angleterre and point applique. It was made in Brussels. … The veil … was held in place by a half coronet of orange blossoms. The train was the regulation court length, five yards. It was fastened to the shoulders about five inches below the neck band, and fell in double box pleats from top to bottom. Down both sides and across the lower edge it was bordered with a two inch embroidery of pearls and silver small rose leaves, formed of finest seed pearls and apparently growing from a vine of silver, which at three inch intervals was tied into a true lover's knot, composed the designs.

The newspapers, of course, also paid attention to the clothes worn by the ushers and the bridesmaids. The ushers:

Wore black frock coats, trousers of light shade, low cut white vests, white puff scarfs and shoes of patent leather. Boutonnieres adorned the left lapels of their coats, while in their scarfs they wore the Duke's presentation pins.

The bridesmaids were most expensively and carefully attired:

Their gowns were made as follows: Ivory white satin was the material, trimmed with sky-blue satin. The skirts were full and untrimmed and broad sash-like streamers of sky-blue satin ribbon reached nearly to the lower edge. The ivory satin appeared again in the bodices, which were close-fitting and finished with full long sleeves. There was a broad waistband of sky blue satin and over the shoulders, crossing surplice fashion in the front, was a Marie Antoinette Fichu of lace. A broad band of blue velvet, clasped with pearls, encircled the throat inside the slightly V shaped neck.

Each bridesmaid also wore a hat:

Each [hat] was of royal blue velvet, broad brimmed, crowned and trimmed with sky blue. The six ostrich plumes fastened at one side were

In this sketch the bridesmaids can be clearly seen along with the lavish floral decorations inside the church.

of blue, as were the large coquilles of satin ribbon filling the back of the caught up brim, and the twist and rosette of chiffon encircling the crown. They carried large bouquets of white roses and lilies of the valley, and wore on their left arms baskets filled with violets, daisies and red roses.

Consuelo's mother, of course, wanted to outshine all the other female guests and her dress was reported, much to her satisfaction, at great length in all the newspapers. She wore:

A superb gown of ciel blue satin. The skirt was of the immense flare pattern now so fashionable, while the bodice had a tight fitting coat back, with two box pleats immediately below the waist. The gown was elaborately trimmed with Russian sable and cream applique lace, while a handsome vest of white mousseline de sole embroidered in silver and pearls adorned the waist.

Thousands of New Yorkers witnessed the spectacle. Alva read, with satisfaction in the press the next day, about the 'amazing throng that covered both sidewalks of 5th Avenue for three blocks in both directions.' The newspaper the *World* was somewhat unkind in the image it drew of the crowds outside the church. They were described as:

> Young women, old women, pretty women, ugly women, fat women, thin women all struggling and pushing and squeezing to break through police lines. ... All quarrelling with one another.

The police estimated the crowd to have been between 6,000 and 7,000. There were 200 policemen on duty. The newspaper said that when the ceremony was over and the crowd finally dispersed 'the policemen, worn out in mind and body, returned to their precincts.' This was all very different from the sedate deference shown to the nobility in England and the relatively reserved nature of the English press at that time.

Alva was determined that the wedding was one which society would remember and speak of for months to come. The church was, therefore, excessively filled with flowers and foliage. There were displays of ferns, pink and white chrysanthemums and red and gold autumn leaves:

> Each pew of the middle aisle had at its outer end a huge floral ball, supported on a standard and topped by a feathery palm. These balls of roses were alternately pink and white.

As well as magnificent flowers, Consuelo's mother also ensured there was a 'full symphony orchestra of sixty pieces' inside the church. It was they and the organist who provided the music for the wedding. The bride walked up the aisle to the 'Lohengrin' wedding march. There was a fifty strong choir and the first hymn sung was 'O perfect love' which was perhaps inappropriate given that the bride and groom did not love each other.

The wedding breakfast

Sunny and his new bride left the church at 1:05 p.m. and were taken in a Vanderbilt carriage to Mrs Vanderbilt's New York home, at 72nd Street and Madison Avenue. As Consuelo descended from the carriage and started to walk away, the Duke inadvertently trod on the train of her dress. She stopped walking and turned round and smiled at him. He hurried to her side somewhat red in the face.

The number of guests at the Wedding Breakfast was far smaller than in the church. They included the bishops who performed the marriage ceremony, Bishop Potter and Bishop Littlejohn, members of the British Embassy and Governor Morton and his family. Each guest was given 'a silver souvenir vase containing wedding cake'. The guests were entertained by an orchestra, different from the one that had played at the wedding and a band. The *World* newspaper commented:

> A Hungarian band was in the upper hallway, and the decorations were superb. ... In the principle room of the mansion ... the Duke and Duchess stood beneath a beautiful floral wedding bell [to receive their guests].

This particular floral display was made up of Lilies of the Valley and was eight foot in circumference.

The guests dined extremely well. They were offered quite a cosmopolitan menu:

Essence of Clovis
Hors d'Oeuvres
Oeufs a la Bourguignonne
Bass a la Russe
Filet mignon aux champignons frais
Pomme de Terre a la Sultana
Pate de foie Gras encroute
Cailles Egyptienne
Salad Florentine
Glace Duchesses
Petits fours & Raisins de Serre
Café, Champagne and Chateau La Rose '77

Alva took every opportunity to make the wedding a reportable success. In summarising the day the American newspapers concluded that it had been a wedding of considerable magnificence and spectacle. Less pleasing for Alva, however, the American newspapers left their readers in no doubt that the Duke had married Consuelo for her dowry.

The English newspapers also reported on the wedding of Sunny and Consuelo in great detail but in a way that left their readers in no doubt that America was the land of excess. The report of the wedding appeared in *The Times* on 7 November, the day after the wedding. The reporter described Consuelo as a 'tall, slight, dark, attractive girl.' He went on to say that the 'Church, artificially lighted at noonday, was a bewildering mass of flowers and brilliant costumes.' The reporter noted that 'nearly all the best known people in New York were there, Astors, Duers, Goelets, Wilsons, Jays, Whitneys, Winthrops, and many more social celebrities.' Queen Victoria and the Prince of Wales both sent congratulatory telegrams which were read out during the wedding breakfast.

The Times reported in slightly shocked tones that the cost of the wedding amounted to £80,000, 'including the Bride's Trousseau.' The reporter was clearly struck by the excessive nature of all aspects of the wedding. He wrote:

> At the bride's home the floral decorations were magnificent. It was estimated that the chrysanthemum blossoms, if piled up, would equal in bulk an ordinary haystack, and the roses, if placed from end to end, would extend over a distance of eight miles. Twenty thousand sprays of lilies of the valley were used.

He was also fascinated by the amount of jewellery given to Consuelo as wedding gifts. It was noted that 'one of the Duke's gifts to the bride [was] a girdle of gold set with diamonds.' He then went on to list other items of jewellery given by the wealthy guests:

A necklace of pearls and diamonds set in antique gold and enamel.

The famous string of pearls formerly belonging to her mother.

A square cut emerald set in a ring with a diamond either side.

A turquoise and diamond marquise ring.

A blue enamel pendant watch set with diamonds.

A pendant heart encrusted with diamonds.

> A pearl brooch – the pearls forming the body of a swan while the neck and wings [were] carried out in diamonds.

Mrs William Astor gave Consuelo 'a purse of golden mesh, the fastening set with turquoises and diamonds.' Mrs W.T. Wilson gave her 'a pair of solid Louis XVI gold vases about six inches in height.' *The Times* reporter concluded:

> I suppose that no American or Anglo-American wedding ever excited so much interest among people of all sorts and conditions, nor was any such ceremony in this city [New York] ever so splendid and elaborate.

Alva was delighted.

The honeymoon

Sunny and his new bride had an extensive honeymoon travelling in Europe but they spent the first couple of days as husband and wife at one of the Vanderbilt residences called 'The Idle Hour' in Oakdale, Long Island. They travelled by train to 'The Idle Hour' and again this journey was reported in great detail in the press. Consuelo 'wore a velvet dress, with a blue silk and lace front, a short fur jacket and a black Gainsborough hat with white feathers.' When the train pulled in at the station, where the carriage should have been waiting, a huge crowd of women had gathered to see the newly married couple. The Duke and Duchess descended from the train and were immediately surrounded by women all of whom talked about them as if they were not even there, commenting on their clothes and general appearance. There were several impertinent comments on how the groom appeared to be smaller than the bride. As their carriage had not appeared they were forced to walk down the road to the house. The onlookers followed them on foot and on bicycle, all the time talking freely about the newlyweds who were both acutely embarrassed. The weather was foggy and the road muddy and this was far from an ideal end to their wedding day.

After their first week of married life at the aptly named 'The Idle Hour' the honeymoon took on an international aspect. On 16 November they boarded the steamer 'Fulda' and sailed out of New York harbour bound for Gibraltar. Consuelo likened the ship to a small cargo boat, lacking in the usual luxuries. She commented that 'there were no beauti-fully decorated suites, no Ritz restaurant, no cinema and no radio.' They were given the Captain's suite, which Consuelo said 'was gloomy and boasted but a minimum of comfort.' She was, however, a good sailor and coped well with the rough crossing. Unhappily the Duke did not fare so well and suffered bouts of sea-sickness. Given there were passenger ships sailing regularly between America and Europe it remains a mystery as to why the newlyweds travelled in this economic way.

The boat arrived in Gibraltar on 25 November and Sunny decided that they would stay for a few days before starting the rest of their tour. Their itinerary included Madrid, Seville, Granada, the French Riviera, Rome, and Brindisi with the final destination being Egypt.

Throughout the honeymoon there were many social engagements. In Madrid, on 4 December 1895, they were invited to a dinner hosted by Sir Henry Drummond-Wolff, the British Ambassador.[2] Consuelo said that Drummond-Wolff was 'charming and courteous.' There she also met Lord Rosebery, who was at that time the leader of the Liberal Party. She believed Rosebery to be a 'brilliant man' but in possession of quite 'a caustic wit.' They were also honoured by an invitation from the Span-ish royal family and whilst in Madrid they were presented at Court to Queen Maria Christina at the Palacio Real. When not meeting royalty or dignitaries, the couple filled their time by visiting galleries, museums and cathedrals. All in all they spent fourteen days in Spain, the last of which was spent travelling by train to France. Arriving in Monte Carlo on 7 December they stayed at the Hotel de Paris.

Later in her life Consuelo looked back on this holiday with some disap-pointment and it would seem from her memoirs that the honeymoon only served to teach each to be disappointed in the other. In these early days of married life she was certainly critical of her husband. Sunny, despite being a slim man, enjoyed fine food. Somewhat undiplomatically he told Con-suelo 'considering that it is the only pleasure one can count on having three times a day, every day of one's life, a well-ordered meal is of prime impor-tance.' Consuelo felt that he spent far too much time discussing the merits of dinner and not always with her, but often with the maitre d'hôtel. They were clearly discovering that they did not relish each other's company.

From Monte Carlo the couple travelled to Rome where unaccounta-bly Consuelo found herself exhausted and doctors were summoned. Rest was ordered and so whilst she stayed at the hotel the Duke explored the antique shops of the city; an activity he enjoyed.

Winston once joked that had Sunny not been born to be an aristocrat he could have made his way in the world as a jockey. He was a fine and fearless horseman but this was a dangerous joke as he was also sensitive about his small stature. In his reply the Duke retorted that if that had been the case he would be found running an old curiosity shop. So it was no surprise to find him rummaging through Rome's antique shops. He also loved art and made a number of purchases. Without sufficient funds, however, he had to send a telegram back to Mr Angas, his land agent at Blenheim, to arrange funds to be sent to a Roman bank.

From Rome, Consuelo and Sunny went to Naples and from there on to Egypt. On 11 January 1895 they were reported to be staying at Shepheard's Hotel in Cairo. They travelled slowly by boat along the Nile, stopping to view the sites by donkey. From Cairo they sailed to Paris where they rented an apartment in the Hotel Bristol. This honeymoon should have been a great adventure completed for the most part in comfort and ease but Consuelo it seems was in no mood to count her blessings. Her mood did not improve in Paris where she was annoyed to find that it was her husband who chose her clothes at the well-known House of Worth. He also oversaw the purchase of jewels for his wife, including a dog collar of pearls that had nineteen rows and diamond clasps. She later remarked that this necklace was most uncomfortable to wear. Nothing seemed to please Consuelo on this trip but perhaps that was because her account of the honeymoon was written in later life, long after her separation and divorce from the Duke, indeed long after he had died.[3]

If the honeymoon had many negative results, one positive result which Consuelo later mentioned was that she had secured a small hold on her husband's heart. Perhaps the trip was not as unhappy as her memoirs portray.

On 29 March they landed at Dover and travelled on to London by train. At the station they found an expectant group of family and friends waiting to welcome them home. The group included Sunny's mother, Lady Albertha Hamilton, two of his sisters Norah and Lilian, his aunt, the formidable Lady Sarah Wilson, his best man Ivor Guest, Lady Randolph Churchill and his cousin Winston. It was a happy occasion particularly for the Duke. Consuelo, who wanted to impress his family, noted she 'felt the scrutiny of many eyes and hoped that [her] hat was becoming and that [her] furs were fine enough to win approval.' Eager to please she was showing her youthful age. Rather poignantly she realised that her husband was home but she was not and that 'the precarious hold [she] had … secured in his life and affections might easily become endangered.' Clearly there was some affection between the young couple, but sadly not enough.

Later that evening whilst at dinner with the assembled company Consuelo's new mother-in-law, Albertha quietly complained that she had been unable to attend the wedding as her son had refused to pay her passage. Apart from this unfortunate comment Albertha treated her new daughter-in-law with kindness and talked to her with genuine interest. Albertha had returned to Blenheim when her son had inherited the title and had run the household on his behalf. Now she would have to make a place for Consuelo. This would not be difficult for Albertha as Blenheim held few good memories for her and it was intolerably cold in winter.

The early days in London after their return were spent in a busy round of family introductions and social engagements. On her second morning Consuelo met Fanny, the Dowager Duchess, who was the Duke's grandmother. They met at the Dowager's town house in Grosvenor Square. In some respects Fanny was responsible for the marriage as she had been amongst those who had advised Sunny to 'marry well' by which of course she meant 'money'. The following day Consuelo met more of the Hamilton side of the family, dining at Hampden House, the London residence of the Duke of Abercorn.[4] The Duke of Abercorn was a kindly man and made Consuelo most welcome joking with her, 'I see the future Churchills will be both tall and good looking.' He was right, Consuelo's two sons both inherited the Vanderbilt height and came to tower over their father who was more Hamilton in stature.

Another of the Duke's aunts was the Marchioness of Lansdowne. She was a woman of character and vivacity and, even better, she was fond of her nephew. Lady Lansdowne had great social influence stemming from her title and wealth but also from the fact that her husband, Lord Lansdowne, was in 1896, the secretary of State for War and previously had been the Viceroy of India. Invitations to the magnificent Lansdowne House in Berkeley Square were coveted by the best of London society. She took a close interest in her nephew and her new daughter-in-law. She genuinely hoped they would be happy. She was, therefore, a useful ally for Consuelo. Lady Lansdowne spent some time acquainting Consuelo with the social expectations of her new position. It was kindly meant and the nineteen-year old from America certainly needed to learn quickly so she could navigate her way through the nobility of Britain. Sunny was not only acquainted with the great and the good, he was also related to many of them by birth and marriage. One of his cousins was the Duke of Roxburghe whilst another was Lord Wimborne. He was also on very good terms with the Royal family. Through the Churchills and the Hamiltons, Consuelo now belonged to two of the most influential families in Britain. They had great expectations of the young American Duchess.

The honeymoon was not, however, quite over. The young couple were expected at Blenheim and their arrival was eagerly anticipated by the townsfolk of Woodstock. As early as 30 March 1896, when they had just arrived at Dover, preparations were underway at Woodstock to welcome

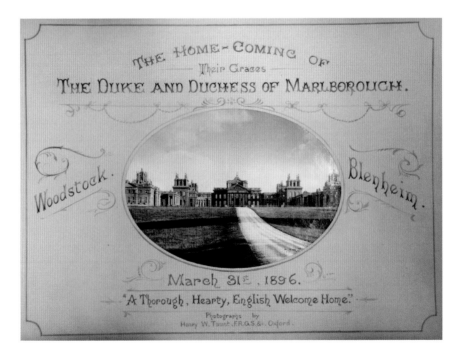

The Fronstipiece of the photograph album which shows the homecoming of Sunny and his new bride. The photographs, taken by Henry Taunt, were placed in an album and given as a gift to Sunny and Consuelo.

The Frontispiece of the photograph album given as a gift to Sunny and Consuelo from the Estate Tenants. This ablum contained photographs of the Duke's tenants who were photographed by Henry Taunt.

the Duke and his new Duchess home. The good people of Woodstock planned to meet the train when it arrived at 3:00 p.m. Consuelo was to be presented with a bouquet by the children of the National School and Sunny was to be given an illuminated address from the Mayor, Mr W.P. Clarke, on behalf of the town. At the Town Hall a formal welcome with speeches was planned after which the townspeople would follow the carriage up to the Palace to see the couple home. All this and more duly happened.

As the train drew into the Woodstock station, the Duke and Duchess saw that a red carpet had been laid along the platform and standing there waiting to greet them were the Mayor and all the Councillors, suitably attired for the occasion. They were welcomed with all due solemnity. Outside the station there were crowds of people and children, who had been given the day off school. There was also an Estate carriage but it was not the Estate horses that pulled the carriage to the Town Hall but the Estate workers. This was a long-held tradition and a very practical

The homecoming procession reaches the Palace. Note the servants who have climbed out of one of the windows to see the Duke and his new Duchess.

way to welcome Sunny and his new wife. The route was lined with well-wishers from Woodstock and the nearby villages, who had turned out to see them. Of course their livelihood depended on this young couple but the local people were also following a time-honoured tradition in giving such a warm welcome to 'their' Duke and Duchess.

At the Palace all the servants were waiting to greet them, dressed immaculately in their uniforms. Also waiting were many of Sunny's tenants. They had commissioned a very special gift for him to mark this auspicious occasion. Henry Taunt, a respected Oxford photographer, had taken photographs of the tenants in their best clothes. These photographs were placed in a leather bound album decorated with silver. Inside was a beautifully illuminated page wishing the Duke and his new wife every happiness.

On the steps of the Palace Sunny made a brief speech of thanks before he and his new wife went inside. At last they were home, although they

Sunny and Consuelo's bedroom.

could not sleep in the bedrooms usually occupied by the Duke and Duchess as they were still being decorated.

The first year of married life

Consuelo and Sunny spent their first year of married life dividing their time between London and Blenheim. At Blenheim he got on with the business of running the Estate whilst she got to know the servants, the Estate workers, tenants and the people who lived in the villages nearby – Woodstock, Bladon, Combe, Stonesfield, Wootton-by-Woodstock and Hanborough. For Consuelo there was much to learn about the running of a great house. She had of course grown up surrounded by splendor with a large number of servants to attend to her needs, but now she had to direct affairs, at least inside the Palace. She was very young and American so there were of course some adjustments required.

There were approximately forty servants working inside the Palace when Sunny brought his bride home for the first time. Consuelo quickly learnt their names, their characters and their standing in the house. The most important servants at that time, at least inside the Palace were: Mr Hardy, the Butler, a man of the highest authority amongst the household servants. He had his own set of rooms in the Undercroft.[5] Mr Rungay, the Chief Electrician, was well paid and treated with a certain amount of awe by the other servants as he was a man of science. He lived in Engineer's Cottage, which in more recent times has been the Butler's house. Mrs Rimand, the Housekeeper, was a very sensible, hard working woman with considerable status in the household. She had a suite of rooms in the mezzanine area, a floor sandwiched between two principles floors in the Palace and Mr Long, the Head Footman, who lived right at the top of the Palace in Workshop Heights, where he had a room of his own. Workshop Heights housed the male servants who worked inside the Palace. It was a large dormitory-like area but with a small number of separate bedrooms for the more senior servants.

At that time there were approximately thirty-five servants working outside, their numbers fluctuating according to need. Mr Whillans was the Head Gardener, Mr Longworth oversaw the Waterworks, Mr Corbett was the Head Forester, Mr Russell was in charge of the stables and Mr Robertson was the Head Gamekeeper. Of these outside employees Consuelo had most to do with Mr Whillans. He was responsible for the beauty of the gardens, growing food for the household and the flowers required to decorate the Palace.[6]

Consuelo and Sunny left Blenheim in May to go to London for the season. In London they lived in what Consuelo called a 'tiny house' in South Audley Street which they rented for May, June and July. They attended dinners, receptions and balls. They went to the opera and the theatre. During the day they would drive to Ranelagh or Roehampton or Hurlingham. Sunny also attended the House of Lords and at times Consuelo listened in the Peeresses Gallery.

Sunny, who had spent most of his life watching the pennies, now had the wherewithal to live in a way that he felt fitted his station. For a start he could not resist purchasing the very smartest modes of transport. In 1896 he bought a Mail Phaeton carriage which had a hood above the seat and behind it a platform for the groom. The groom in question happened to be a rather small man who went by the name of Tiger. He also purchased a crimson State Coach. When travelling in this the coachman wore a livery of crimson cloth with silver braid on which was embroidered the double-headed eagles of the Duke's coat of arms. The coachman also wore a white wig under his hat and had white breeches and silk stockings. Over all this the coachman wore a red coat with shoulder capes. So even though they lived in a relatively small rented house, the Duke and Duchess cut quite a dash as they travelled around London.

During this first year of married life they were often in the company of royalty. Both Sunny and the Prince of Wales were interested in horse racing so they would both regularly attend, with their respective wives, the main races of which the most grand was Ascot in June. On 3 July the Prince of Wales and the Duke were at Newmarket where they saw Sunny's horse Barabbas come fourth. On 11 September he was in Doncaster with the Prince of Wales for the races. His horse, Barabbas was running in the Rous Plate for two year olds but on this occasion did not win.

There were many social occasions when Sunny and Consuelo were in the company of various members of the Royal Household. On 29 May they were part of the royal party which stayed at Hatfield House and went on to the Bath and West Society's Show at St Albans. In this party were the Prince and Princess of Wales, the Princesses Victoria and Maud and Prince Charles of Denmark. Also in the party were the Marquess and Marchioness of Salisbury, the Marquess and Marchioness of Londonderry and many other noble ladies and Members of Parliament. On 11 June 1896 they attended a fundraising dinner for Guy's Hospital at the Imperial Institute in London. The Prince of Wales presided over the event. Consuelo was on the Reception Committee, with many other noble ladies, which organised the event. On 13 July the Queen invited them to a garden party at Buckingham Palace. This was a large affair and all the great and good attended. Later that month, on 18 July the Queen invited them to a small dinner at Windsor Castle where they had the quiet and space to actually talk at length with Her Majesty.

Royalty also visited Blenheim. On 23 November the Prince and Princess of Wales, with a large entourage, spent a few days at the Palace. Their visit was enlivened with many forms of entertainment. There was of course shooting in the Park.

The Duchess took some of the party into Oxford to visit the Bodleian Library, Christ Church and Magdalene College. On 26 November there was a ball in the Long Library. The following evening there was a

The Royal shooting party, 1896, outside High Lodge. Back row from left to right:-
Earl of Gosford, Lady Emily Kingscote, Hon. Sidney Greville, Mr. G. Curzon, General
Ellis, Sir Samuel Scott, Lord Londonderry, Lady Helen Stewart, Lady Lilian Spencer-
Churchill (Sunny's sister), Mr. Grenfell, Prince Charles of Denmark, Viscount Curzon.
Middle row:- Earl of Chesterfield, Lady Randolph Churchill, Duchess of Marlborough,
the Princess of Wales, Mr. H. Chaplin, the Prince of Wales, Mrs. George Curzon,
Marchioness of Londonderry, Princess Victoria, Princess Charles of Denmark. Front
Row:- Lady Sophie Scott, Duke of Marlborough, Viscountess Curzon.

torchlight procession of approximately 1,000 people across the Park to a gigantic bonfire which was near the Monument to the 1st Duke of Marlborough. The royal party, assorted nobility and the people of Woodstock were then treated to a magnificent display of fireworks followed by an amusing fancy dress cycle parade.

The distinguished visitors left Blenheim on the morning of 28 November, their carriages pulling away from the north steps at 10:25 a.m. precisely. The royal party were cheered as they travelled through Woodstock, escorted by Sunny in his position of Lieutenant of the Queen's Own Oxfordshire Hussars and the Woodstock Troop. The Duke continued with the royal party all the way to Oxford Station although at Yarnton the Oxford Troop of the Yeomanry took over guard and escort duty. The entire route to Oxford was lined with well-wishers anxious to catch a glimpse of the Royal family and their own Duke. The young couple clearly moved in the finest social circles and life at this time was good.

During their first year of married life they fulfilled many obligations of a charitable nature. On 14 May 1896 the Duke hosted a fundraising dinner at the Whitehall Rooms, Hotel Metropole in London to raise money for the National Orthopaedic Hospital in Great Portland Street. The Duchess attended the dinner as did the Lord Mayor and Lady Mayoress of London, along with various dignitaries and their wives. The hospital had been enlarged and £1,650 remained of the costs to pay for construction work and the equipment of the new extension. On 24 October Sunny presided over the Autumnal Assembly of Homes for Little Boys in the Royal Albert Hall. Consuelo presented the prizes.

They were also called upon to open fêtes and country shows. On 4 June the Duchess opened a Garden Fête and sale of work at Frognal Park in Hampstead. This event was organised by the Ladies Samaritan Society and the funds were intended for the North Eastern Hospital for Children. Later that month, accompanied by her husband, she re-opened the Rose Show and Bazaar at the Queen's Hall, Langham Place, in London. It had originally been opened by the Duchess of Connaught.

In amongst all the fund raising events and royal visits of their first year of marriage they also attended to quite ordinary affairs. However, even if their actions were commonplace, they were reported in the newspapers because they were the celebrities of their day. Such was their fame that *The Times* reported that on 3 August Sunny had purchased a two-year old Jersey heifer at auction for 53 guineas. The newspaper led its readers to believe that this was no ordinary heifer. It was in fact from the 'celebrated Jersey herd of Sir James Blyth' and the animal cost the Duke the princely sum of 55 guineas! The heifer rejoiced in the name Snowflake.

Not all animals owned by Sunny were looked upon with the same pleasure as Snowflake. Deer in the Park at Blenheim were a constant annoyance to him and throughout 1896 he paid Mr Huckins 15 shillings to keep the deer out of the Pleasure Grounds. Mr Huckins worked for many years keeping the deer at a suitable distance from the immaculate gardens. The ha-ha built by 'Capability' Brown in the 1760s was no obstacle for them. Sunny eventually 'banned' deer from the park during

Consuelo with her two sons, Bert and Ivor. Bert sits on Consuelo's right and Ivor on her left.

the First World War. He said they ate the bark off trees, trampled the flowers, chased visitors and even swam in the lake!

Outside of their formal social commitments Consuelo and Sunny found time to visit friends and relatives in London. In July they went to see the Wimborne side of the family. This was the family of Ivor Guest, one of the Duke's closest friends and first cousin. Their principal family residence was an enormous house, Canford Manor in Dorset, which is now a private school. In September they also went aboard. Their destination was unknown and all *The Times* could say on the matter was: 'The Duke and Duchess of Marlborough left from London yesterday for the continent.' The 'yesterday' in question was 24 September.

So all in all they had a very busy and socially successful 1896 as husband and wife. As an added bonus, by the end of the year Consuelo was pregnant. Their first child, a son, was born in September 1897. Sunny's heir was named John after the 1st Duke of Marlborough, Albert after Queen Victoria's husband, and Edward after the Prince of Wales, who was one of the baby's godparents or sponsors as they were called at the time. The baby was christened on 16 October 1897 in the Chapel Royal, St James' Palace. The Prince of Wales gave to Consuelo a gift for the infant; a gold cup bearing on one side the Prince's coat of arms and on the other those of the Duke of Marlborough.

Ivor, their second child, was named after the Duke's closest friend and confident, Ivor Guest and of course his second name was Sunny's own Christian name, Charles. Ivor was christened on 21 November 1898, also in the Chapel Royal at St James' Palace, but this time without royal guests.

The early years of their married life were by all accounts a success. They were blessed with, as Consuelo said, an heir and a spare.

3

Everyday life for the Duke

A life on the move

Sunny, both as a single and married man, lived a peripatetic life. Most of his time was divided between London, Sysonby Lodge and Blenheim, but at times he would visit friends on their estates scattered around the country for house parties. The archive at Chatsworth holds the secrets of a memorable fancy dress ball attended by the Duke, Consuelo and many other noble ladies and gentlemen in 1897. For many years Warwick Castle had a waxwork of Sunny on display as part of a 'weekend party' reconstruction at the Castle.

The Duke's movements and activities were regularly reported in both the London and local newspapers. On 14 January 1899 *Jackson's Oxford Journal* reported:

> The Duke of Marlborough entertained the Mayor and Corporation of Woodstock, and the Mayor and Town Clerk of Oxford, to dinner at Blenheim Palace, on Saturday evening last.
>
> The Duke and Duchess of Marlborough left Blenheim Palace on Monday for Chatsworth. Their Graces go to Sysonby Lodge, Melton Mowbray, early next week, for the remainder of the hunting season.

This life of moving between houses, their own and those belonging to friends and relations, was entirely normal for members of the aristocracy. It was also in keeping with the traditions of the day for the movements of the aristocracy to be reported in the newspapers. They were

The Duke was a confident horseman, here photographed in later life on horseback riding through Woodstock.

the celebrities of their time. Given that in his early years as Duke, most travelling was done slowly by horseback or carriage to and from railway stations, it is surprising just how much travelling he did. He was rarely in one place for long. It was fortunate that he was an excellent horseman and had no objections to rail travel. Travelling by ship was another matter as he frequently became seasick.

The train was the most common mode of transport at the time for long distances and it was fortunate that the 7th Duke, had brought the railway to Woodstock. Newspaper reports, however, tell us that Sunny would not always travel to Woodstock station but often returned home via Hanborough, Kidlington or Oxford. After arriving at whichever of the local stations, his mode of transport onwards depended on the weather. If the weather was fine he would ride rather than be driven in his carriage or, later in his life, in his car. On one occasion he sent the carriage away and walked. It was 16 March 1901 when the Estate Clerk noted: 'His Grace arrived at Kidlington station at 6.42pm and walked up to the Palace. Mr Winston Churchill was with His Grace.' What a change of circumstances for the two young men who not long before had seen action together in the Boer War and now were occupied in a pleasant walk across the Duke's fields in fine weather.

The 9th Duke became very well acquainted with the train services between Blenheim and London as he travelled constantly between the two. In fact sometimes he would leave Blenheim in the morning for a function in London 'by the 8.35am at Hanborough Station' and return 'by the 6.40pm at Kidlington' and think nothing of the miles covered and the time spent travelling. He also travelled frequently between Blenheim and his other estate, Sysonby, near Melton Mowbray. The Duke did not travel light. Freddie Birkenhead (F.E. Smith, 1st Earl of Birkenhead's son) wrote in his father's biography:

> The Duke also owned a hunting lodge, Sysonby, at Melton Mowbray, which he would visit from time to time with the more modest retinue of the Groom of the Chambers, two Footmen, three Housemaids, three in the kitchen, an Odd Man, the Stud Groom, the Second Horseman, and stable helpers. This army was conveyed both ways in a special train.

The station he used depended on the timetable but being a Duke the railway companies would oblige by making a special stop for His Grace or for important visitors staying at the Palace. On 31 August 1901 Mr Josiah Hine, Estate Clerk, wrote in his diary: 'His Grace returned to Blenheim from Harrogate arriving about 3.30pm. Great Central stopped the train at Kidlington for His Grace's convenience.' The reason he had to return to the Palace swiftly was because the Crown Prince of Germany had requested a visit on that same day. Hine continued:

> His Imperial Highness [arrived] at Blenheim Woodstock Station by Special Train about 7.45pm. His Grace met the distinguished visitor at the station and drove through the town to Blenheim. There was much cheering at the station by the crowd of people assembled there.

Royal visits
Royalty visited the Palace often in the Duke's early years at Blenheim, a most frequent visitor being the Prince of Wales. The Prince and his

entourage would travel up from London by special train then on to the Palace by a long line of carriages with escorts provided by the local yeomanry, in great pomp and circumstance. The Prince's first visit was in 1896 when the Duke had only been married a few months. Arthur Balfour, the future Prime Minister, accompanied him on this first visit and was rather disparaging about the journey and wrote as if the special treatment they received was to be endured rather than enjoyed:

> We came down by special train [and] were received with illuminations, guards of honour, cheering [crowds] and other follies, went through agonies about our luggage, but finally settled down placidly enough.

These royal visits stopped after Sunny's separation from Consuelo.

The Duke's preferred mode of transport was always the horse and he was a most accomplished horseman. His hunting horses were Greys, – famously painted by Sir Alfred Munnings, – and his carriage horses were Bays. The horses were kept in the stables in Great Court and in the village of Bladon near Home Farm. The number of horses stabled at Blenheim would increase by over double when there were guests and house parties at the Palace. The Duke's great friend F.E. Smith would ride over to Blenheim with his family from his home in the nearby village of Charlton, which was 12 miles from Blenheim. F.E. usually brought four horses for himself, two for his wife, two ponies for his children and three horses for the grooms.

F.E. visited often so the Blenheim grooms grew to know his horses well. He also got into the habit of using the stables as if they were an extra home for his horses and would leave them there if he was in the area and not actually visiting the Duke. In March 1900 F.E. wrote to the land agent, Mr Angas:

> My Dear Angas
>
> I am having two horses brought over to Blenheim, as I am going to ride about all day on Sunday.
>
> Can you find a room for the man in the servants' quarters, as it is rather a long way for him to go up and down from the village?
>
> Yours Sincerely
>
> FE

On another occasion when F.E. and his family were visiting, F.E. brought even more horses than usual. The Duke, when he found out, complained to one of his grooms:

> Whose are all these damned horses?
> Lord Birkenhead's Your Grace.
> Lord Birkenhead's? I never heard of such confounded impudence. How long have they been eating their heads off at my expense?

He then stormed up to the Palace and found F.E.: 'You are a damned scoundrel, F.E., a damned horse thieving scoundrel of a gypsy!' and then he burst out laughing. He could never stay angry for long where F.E. was concerned.

The Duke was not so forgiving to those who worked for him if he suspected some sort of negligence, especially where his horses were concerned. On 6 March 1895 he wrote with some anger to Mr Angas about the death of a young filly in the Park. Mr Angas defended himself explaining:

> Your Grace
> I am sorry you should think that the 'handsome boy' filly died from neglect. This is certainly not the case. The filly slipped on ice and drowned.
> I remain your obedient servant
> R.L. Angas

Despite his love of horses the 9th Duke was quick to embrace the latest mode of transport, the automobile. His first motorcar was purchased in 1902 and arrived at Blenheim on 29 May. He enjoyed being driven and driving the car himself, but this was not without its problems. On 23 August 1902, whilst driving into Oxford, he crashed into a horse and trap. The two ladies in the trap were thrown out, both were badly shaken and hurt and he immediately took them to the Radcliffe Infirmary. The ladies had stopped the horse because they knew the horse was frightened of motorcars but he had not expected them to stop. On this occasion the old and new worlds of transport collided with unfortunate results and the horse remained terrified of cars.

In 1910 he had a Wolseley car built for him in Birmingham and once delivered he used it to go on holiday to Italy. He was very pleased with

A view of the Park & Palace from the air. Sunny believed that the paths and narrow roads around the Park were not made for cars or bicycles. They were for horses, horse drawn carriages and for walking.

the car and from the Grand Hotel in Florence he wrote to Mr Angas saying that the car had performed very well before adding, 'the weather in this country is too glorious, nothing but sunshine and not too hot. It is very interesting to see the harvest of grapes being collected.' It was rare for Mr Angas to receive a letter from the Duke that did not contain some instruction about the Blenheim farms or a demand to know what the weather was like in England. Clearly he was in a relaxed mood.

He may have enjoyed driving cars but he insisted that no one was to drive them in Blenheim Park, except himself. No one was allowed to cycle either. This rule about cycling is still enforced today.

Just before he died the Duke purchased a Rolls-Royce Sedanca Limousine Registration number 3721. He obviously had a good eye for the lines of a car as well as a horse!

The Palace and Estate

Wherever he was, the Duke never lost sight of his primary responsibility, which was always for the maintenance and welfare of Blenheim Palace, his family, the Estate, his servants and tenants. This was neither a small nor an easy task and he took his responsibilities most seriously.

One of the responsibilities he felt most keenly was that he should hand over the Palace and Estate to the next generation, in better condition than he had found it in 1892, when his father died. To outward appearances he had at that time, inherited great wealth, a position of power and a life of privilege. Privilege and power he had, but in 1892 he most certainly did not have wealth. By far the largest drain on his finances was the Palace itself. The costs of its upkeep were (and still are) enormous and the problems seemingly never ending. These problems followed him wherever he went, whether he was in London, staying with friends or abroad. In January 1895 he went for a brief holiday to Monte Carlo. The land agent, Mr Angas, wrote giving him a progress report concerning the problem of a sewage leak in the Undercroft at the Palace.

Mr Angas wrote:

> The men have got down to the drain in the Eastern corridor in the Palace and we find it in a very bad state indeed. … The sewage leaks out quite fast and the smell is very bad. … When you come down you must not go to the Palace.

In February 1895 the problem was still unresolved. By this time he was in London where on 7 February Mr Angas wrote:

> The weather here is dreadfully severe and much work is at a standstill. I do not know if we had found a second cess pool in the Palace when you were here on 28th January. We found it under the Housekeeper's room. It was not full but had about 2ft of poisonous stuff in it, no wonder Blenheim smelt.

It was not just the cost of maintaining and repairing his 300 year old home but the Duke also had numerous worries concerning his substantial Estate. There were many people living and working on the Estate who needed him to run the Estate in such a way that guaranteed their

Whenever the Duke was in residence his flag would be hoisted above the Palace. When he was away the flag would be taken down. Today the same flag flies when the Duke is in residence. When he is away however the Cross of St George is hoisted into place.

livelihoods. There were also various family members all reliant on his solvency. A New York reporter was quick to highlight the financial commitments that would face the young Duke noting on 11 November 1892:

> The Dukedom will be the heaviest dowagered title in the peerage. The widows of the 6th and 7th Dukes are still alive. Next comes the Marchioness of Blandford, the late Duke's first wife, and lastly the present Duchess. The jointures of these four will add to the drain upon the revenues of the Estate.

His grandmother, Fanny, had an allowance, less tax of £1,208.6s.8d. per annum. His mother, Albertha had an annual allowance of £2,000 paid quarterly. It was not just the Dowagers who had to be provided for; he also had to give generous allowances to his three sisters. His two older sisters Lady Lilian and Lady Norah each received £400 a year paid half yearly and Frances his third sister received almost £600 per year until she was married when it was reduced to match that of her older sisters.

When he inherited the Estate in 1892 it was running at a loss. Mr Angas who was under great strain often wrote to the Duke informing him of this fundamental problem. Added to this was the fact that Sunny wanted to limit and control the flow of funds. This led to short term financial embarrassments which only compounded the overall problem of expenditure being higher than income. On 1 April 1895 he was in London and received the following note from Mr Angas:

> Our expenses are sure to be much more than our receipts until the rent day in June, and when the rent day arrives we are always several thousands overdrawn at the Bank. This has been the case ever since you succeeded.

Mr Angas found the new, young Duke unrealistic in his expectations concerning possible economies and the limited amount of funds with which he expected him to run the Estate. On 10 January 1895 he wrote:

> Your Grace
>
> You state that £300 per week is the maximum amount I have authority to ask Lloyds for, as this is so we shall be very much overdrawn at Gilletts from time to time, which is just what I understood was to be avoided. This overdraft will be caused by, for instance, this month payments having to be made for Income Tax, Licenses on account to different Collectors in some 20 different parishes, amounting to £1,200. According to your instructions I shall receive from Lloyds this month £900 so that when I have paid the wages say £450 out of the £900 there will remain £450 to meet the £1,200 liability.
>
> I remain Your Grace's obedient servant
> R. L. Angas

This problem of a serious lack of funds was only solved by the Duke's marriage to Consuelo Vanderbilt and the very large injection of funds this alliance brought to the Spencer-Churchills.

Forestry and farming

Sunny's Estate was split, as it is today, into areas of forestry and farming. The Duke's foresters, then as now, planted and cared for all kinds of trees: hornbeam, oak, beech, ash, willow and chesnuts. The foresters planted trees that in future could be sold for a profit. They grew trees that provided the wood people needed such as oaks for house building, hornbeam for tools and cogs and willow for cricket bats. During the First World War the Estate provided props for the trenches on the Front line. The Duke and his foresters planted trees for aesthetic reasons and to ensure a future supply of timber. The present Duke and his foresters continue with this tradition. They recently planted over 100 oaks that will be harvested in approximately 180 years time.

Sunny always took a particular interest in the state of the farms on his estate. Home Farm and Park Farm provided for the family and servants. All the other farms were in the hands of tenants. These tenant farms were regularly inspected by the land agent and occasionally by the Duke himself. Both men were always very clear that farms had to be 'clean'; by this they meant free from weeds. Farm buildings and the farm houses had to be maintained in good condition, inside and out. Animals all had to be well-fed and cared for. Most farmers lived up to these high expectations although on occasion they had to be reminded of their responsibilities. Sometimes it was the other way round and the farmers complained to the agent or to the Duke. In 1895 Mr William Ferguson of Woodleys Farm near Woodstock, complained about rabbits:

> My Lord Duke
> I have complained to Mr Angas (the land agent) and sent him a list of my losses this year amounting to £107.18[s].0[d] not including the straw. When I took the farm it was on the distinct understanding that the rabbits was [sic] not to be allowed to damage my crops instead of that the present Steward of Kingswood imported them into the Wood until it is impossible for me to get a living after myself and family slaving all year round.

Mr Ferguson finished by giving notice to leave. The Duke was very aware of the rabbit problem. His keepers were instructed to keep the rabbit population in check and often he and his friends would spend an afternoon or morning dealing with the problem. On one day they managed to shoot 7,500. It is a record that has not been surpassed on the Estate since.

He received many reports from his land agent about the state of his farms and sometimes these reports would concentrate on a particular

Sunny was a keen shot, here seen shooting snipe in the bog by the lake.

aspect such as tenant farmers, who were valued if they managed to maintain their boundaries without 'troubling the Estate too often for timber.'

He spent a considerable amount of time discussing farming with his land agent and indeed haranguing the agent to get the best out of the Home Farms as well as the tenant farms. His attention to detail did not waver even when he was away. In July 1921 whilst on his honeymoon in France, he sent Mr Fitzroy, the then land agent, two postcards. One postcard enquired about the health of the 'Fat Cattle' and the other just said:

Are you attending to the thatching of all hayricks? This work should now be finished if your organisation had been good.
Marlborough.

The Duke's advice was not restricted to hayricks. A few days later on 22 July and still on honeymoon, by that time in Monte Carlo, he wrote again to Fitzroy:

Pray arrange that all cattle get 1lb of ground barley oats etc. as per my letter to you. Matter urgent.
Marlborough

Sunny did his best to promote excellent farming methods by adopting them on his own land and encouraging his tenant farmers to do the same. The one innovation he was not sure about however was the use of tractors. He had a very low opinion of these machines. He felt they would be useless in the spring rains. In the early days he permitted their use only for getting tree roots out of the ground after felling. On 27 April 1910

Sunny and one of his very healthy looking bulls.

the Oxford Steam Plough Company was paid £6 to clear the ground at Round Close near Combe. At the same time the company supplied a ten ton steamroller at 22 shillings and 6 pence a day to maintain the Park roads. The Duke hired the roller for 2 weeks at the beginning of May. By 1922 the Estate had its own tractor. On 17 May 1922 the land agent, then Mr Fitzroy, wrote to his employer: 'Hawkes has been very busy rolling the wheat and for that purpose has been using the tractor.' Other farms on the Estate made use of tractors long before the Duke was won over.

Sunny encouraged local farming in general by supporting and attending as many agricultural shows as possible and hosting a number of them in Blenheim Park. He presented prizes for 'Fat Stock' at the 'Fat Stock Show'. He also presented prizes at numerous shows for best 'filly foal' and best 'colt foal', for best pig and best bull. Often he entered his own animals and produce in such shows. On 13 September 1898 in a show held in the Park he won 1st prize for his 'filly foal' and second prize for his 'colt foal.'

Every year Sunny held a Harvest Thanksgiving luncheon for all his tenant farmers at the Palace. In general there were between forty-six and forty-eight tenant farmers (although the fall in land prices after the First

World War led him to sell a number of farms). The Harvest Thanksgiving was a time to bring all the tenant farmers together. Josiah Hine recorded in his diary the Harvest Thanksgiving of 10 September 1899:

> Luncheon was served at 1.30pm. There were 46 tenants present including Mr Angas. Half had lunch in the Arcade Room with His Grace and the remainder in the Dining Room with Her Grace. The weather although cold was fine and the service [in the Chapel] was a success. After [the] service the tenants assembled in the Long Library where a short organ recital was given, and the tenants had the pleasure of seeing the Marquess of Blandford and Lord Ivor Spencer Churchill.' [The Duke's two young sons.]

When Sunny inherited the Estate in 1892 the finances were in a very poor condition and he tried at that time to sell some farms in order to reduce the deficit but this proved very difficult. In 1894, for example, he instructed his solicitors, Messrs. Milward & Co, to sell land in Ardley and Black Bourton. On 4 July the solicitors wrote to the Duke painting a mixed picture:

> My Lord Duke
>   Yesterday's Sales
>   You will have gathered from our telegram last night that the result was not quite as good as we expected. There was not a bidder of any kind for any one of the four Black Bourton Farms, but I think I shall probably succeed in selling the Rock Farm to the present tenant within a week.

The farm was indeed sold to the tenant for £5,000. The £5,000 whilst useful was not a solution to the ongoing problem. On 23 October of that same year he had to repay a loan to Sir John Jaffray of £25,000. In order to do this he took out another loan from Lloyds Bank who charged 4%!

The financial situation was so dire that Sunny even decided to sell a church. On 29 October 1894 his solicitors sent him a note:

> I will write to Baron Ferdinand Rothschild as to the Living at Waddesdon and will ascertain whether he is willing to negotiate for the purchase. I observe that you will not sell cheap.

It was Sunny's grandfather, the 7th Duke of Marlborough, who sold the land to Baron Rothschild, to build Waddesdon Manor. Baron Rothschild did not purchase the Living.[1]

The agricultural year revolved around the seasons and were marked, not just by the sowing of seeds and the harvest but by many agricultural shows and by the existence of local agricultural societies. In Oxfordshire, as in most counties during the late Victorian period and early Edwardian times, there were many agricultural shows. Many approached the Duke to be their patron and to provide funds to support them. If he agreed to be a patron it meant they could put his name on their headed note paper and that acted as an influential pull for other people of all classes to come to the show or event. It also meant that he was likely to agree to attend the event and give out the prizes, some of which he would have donated. Quite often these agricultural shows were held in Blenheim Park. On 13 September 1898, the Estate Clerk, Josiah Hine, noted that the Flower Show, in the Park, had gone off well despite a little rain at lunchtime. There had been more entries in both livestock and deadstock at this show than the previous year. He also noted that the Duke's Billy Goats had won first and second prize!

In September 1908, the Woodstock Agricultural and Horticultural Association held their dog show in Blenheim Park 'by permission of the Duke of Marlborough'. This was an annual event although that particular year it seemed part of the show was a little disappointing. It was reported in the local newspaper that 'the entry of sporting breeds was not equal to that which had been seen at many of the early shows.'

On 3 May 1912 he received the following letter:

My Lord Duke

As your Grace is aware the Oxfordshire Agricultural Society will hold their show at Witney in May next and I am writing on behalf of the local committee to solicit a subscription from your local fund.

Your Grace, I know, takes an interest in Witney and we are pleased to have you, a considerate land owner, in our district, and it will greatly cheer and encourage us all to see Your Grace's name on our list of subs. When the show was last held at Witney, Your Grace kindly assisted us.

I have the honour to be

My Lord Duke, Your Grace's most obedient Servant

Wm Smith

The Duke contributed £20.

The Estate during the First World War

At no time did Sunny and his farming tenants work harder and under more difficult conditions than they did during the First World War. In 1917 he was made Joint Parliamentary Secretary for Agriculture and Fisheries and so he spent the last two years of the war working in government and in particular in the House of Lords. In Parliament he spoke on agricultural matters such as the difficulties faced by fishermen during the war and the introduction of motorised tractors on farms. He also spoke of the necessity of producing as much food as possible and in April 1918 he donated 500 head of cattle to reduce the shortage of meat. Early in the war he had taken steps to increase food production on the Estate. Areas of grassland in the Park were ploughed up and planted with a variety of crops. The lake was used to produce as much fish as possible. Sheep were used as lawnmowers, vegetables were grown in the formal gardens instead of flowers and deer were banished from the Park.

As the war progressed the shortage of labour to work on the land became a serious problem. There were many women, including the Duchess of Marlborough, who believed that women should take over the jobs left vacant by men who had gone to the front, including farm work, and indeed many women did take over these responsibilities. Surprisingly the Duke was one of many who encouraged women to work on the land. In so doing he inadvertently encouraged great social change, one which he undoubtedly did not anticipate or seek as he was the most traditional of Victorian men.

Throughout the war the land agent, Mr Palmer, made regular inspections of all the tenant farms. Caleb and Job Honour were successful tenants who farmed Sansomes and Weverely Farms. As the war dragged on they both began to struggle and received several sharp warnings from the agent to 'clean' their farms of weeds. This proved very difficult because of the severe shortage of labour. Another successful farmer, James Slatter was warned in 1916 about the condition of his farm and Mr Slatter 'took this ill.' In 1917 the land agent inspected his farm again and reported that Slatter's 'wheat, potatoes and roots look well' but not so his barley. However Mr Palmer finished with a gentle tone by noting: 'This man is doing his best, his brother has gone to the Front.' In 1917 the agent inspected the small holding farmed by F. Castle and noted: 'Castle's son has gone to the front and his pony is getting too old to work.' At the same time Mr Palmer reported that Mr P. Davis, who farmed Akeman Farm, had to sell his 150 sheep when his shepherd was sent to the front.

Despite the severe shortage of labour there is no mention made in the land agent's reports of farmers using women from the Land Corps. Whilst the Duke may have been very enthusiastic about women working on the land it would seem his tenants were not.

The weather man

As a consequence of his fascination with agriculture Sunny developed a corresponding deep interest in the weather that bordered on the obsessive. This was because of the impact the weather could have on the lives of his tenant farmers, his own farms and therefore on the wealth and well-being of all who lived on his estate. Whilst on honeymoon in June 1921, he wrote to his land agent from Nice saying: 'Send me a detailed daily statement of the weather and how much rain from July 1st.' History does not record how his wife felt about this distraction. Mr Fitzroy, the land agent, dutifully sent reports of the weather and precise measurements of rain which in the event amounted to very little as it was a very hot and dry summer.

Letters sent between the various land agents and the Duke were frequent and often showed that the Estate was, from time to time, battered with severe weather. In March 1895 there was a terrible snowstorm, although such storms were not uncommon. Winters were far more severe and summers hotter and dryer than they routinely are today. It was for this reason that Sunny was somewhat obsessed with the weather. His influence rubbed off on his servants, so the land agent and Estate Clerk made a point of recording the weather in their letters and diaries on a daily basis. From these we know that in the year Queen Victoria died, 1901, the weather started dull, foggy, wet and with 'a terribly cold biting NE wind'. January that year ended with a 'very rough wind and cold [with] a little rain'. Altogether a very gloomy month.

The direction of the wind was always important, especially during the shooting season, and was usually included in the notes on the weather. The Duke and his guests would shoot whatever the weather during the season. On 8 January, even though there had been 'a sharp frost during the night' and the temperature was 'much colder' and 'it continued snowing' the Duke spent the afternoon 'shooting pheasants round about the Lince'. On 21 January there was a brief respite in the wind and rain and Josiah Hine, the Estate Clerk, noted that:

> His Grace left Blenheim about 2.30pm and rode into Oxford enroute for Melton. On hearing of the grave condition of her majesty, His Grace came back to Blenheim.
>
> The weather 'continued mild'.

On 22 January Mr Hine recorded in his diary:

> Mild Day
> His Grace shooting at Pinsley [wood}
> Her Majesty Queen Victoria died at Osbourne House, Isle of Wight 6.30pm.

On such a momentous day the first item on the list was the weather! Clearly his obsession with the weather had rubbed off on the Estate Clerk. The Duke and Duchess, of course, attended the Queen's funeral and when they left for Windsor on 31 January, the weather necessitated a carriage.

The impact of the weather on the life of the Estate and the Duke was not always bad. In winter the lake regularly froze enough for him and his family and the people of Woodstock to go ice-skating. Sometimes people were too keen to try out the ice and found themselves in difficulties. On 9 December 1902 two Oxford Undergraduates went through the ice up to their necks. They were rescued with a ladder and rope. But generally it was so cold and the ice so thick that people could skate for several months on the lake. On 23 December 1901 Mr Hine noted in his diary: 'People skating on the lake all day'. On 26 December 1901 he wrote: 'Ice very good indeed'. The lake froze again in 1902 and on 18 February there was an ice hockey match between Oxford and Cambridge played on the frozen lake. It was a draw with two goals each. The next day the thaw set in but the ice was still 4 ½ inches thick!

When the lake froze it was always welcomed as it provided guests staying at the Palace with the opportunity to skate. The Duke always had a large house party for Christmas and New Year. His friends and relations would visit with their families, servants, horses and carriages and fill Blenheim with noise and festive high jinks. A typical guest list included Winston and Jack Churchill, who brought their growing families as did Ivor Guest. Their children signed the guest book as and when they were old enough to do so. The Duke's mother, Albertha, and his sisters, Frances, Lilian and Norah were always invited as was his great friend F.E. Smith. Freddie Birkenhead (F.E's son) wrote a biography of his father and in this he wrote nostalgically of the wonderful Christmas parties at Blenheim and in particular of skating on the lake: 'The great lake was frozen and the woods white with winter... and skates rang on the ice.'

His sister, Eleanor Smith, remembered with great fondness night skating on the lake:

> The lake itself seemed as wide as the sea and moonlight was reflected palely in the darkness of the ice. Torches glared; lanterns darted with the swiftness of fireflies. The clash of skates tinkled as crisply as sleigh bells and the dark figures of the skaters flashed like tiny dolls across the illuminated ice.

The winters were clearly colder when the Duke was alive than they are today. The summers were often extremely hot which concerned him because of the animals and crops. In his heart he was a farmer and a countryman. He was passionately interested in all aspects of agriculture and so was obsessed about the lack of rain in the summer and extreme heat. This was a particular problem in the early summer of 1901. On 11 July 1901 Mr Hine noted: 'Very hot indeed, 86 degrees in the shade'. Thankfully on 13 July he was able to report a 'nice shower of rain'.

Sometimes the weather obliged and smiled on the many and various functions the Duke and Duchess were called upon to attend. On 20 August 1901 they attended two local flower shows and distributed prizes. They were out all day and returned to Blenheim at 7:00 p.m. Mr Hine noted it had been a 'beautifully fine day'. On 13 October that same year there was the traditional Harvest Thanksgiving at the Palace followed by luncheon for the tenants; fifty-two in total. Mr Hine noted, perhaps with some understandable relief: 'The weather was nice and bright and everything passed off well.'

At other times the weather was most disobliging. On 11 September Mr Hine noted:

> Sale of Jerseys [cows] took place at the Cowyards this day. Very wet all morning. …. the attendance was not very large. Luncheon was provided in the cart...

Local affairs, patronage and politics

Sunny was asked to be patron of many associations, and not just agricultural ones:

> The Abb Kettleby Cricket club in Melton Mowbray (he did have a house nearby so perhaps was even able to play himself).
> The Oxfordshire Chess Association.
> The Oxfordshire Agricultural Society.
> The Wolvercote Horticultural Society.
> The Oxfordshire and Buckinghamshire Light Infantry Old Comrades Dinner Club (For this group he was asked to be President of the club and not just patron).

Sunny was a follower of what his descendants call 'the beautiful game' or football and he happily supported various local football clubs. In 1912 he gave 5 shillings to help Stonesfield Football Club buy new equipment. He also enjoyed cricket and Stonesfield Cricket Club often held matches in the Park. His love of cricket stayed with him all his life.

He involved himself in the everyday concerns of the villages and towns on his estate. He was assailed with and endeavoured to solve all sorts of problems. In January 1910 there was a serious issue of the house for the schoolmaster in Stonesfield. The problem was that there was no house; the ratepayers in Stonesfield could not afford to build one and no builder could be found to build one at his own risk. He was away at the time and said he would deal with the matter on his return.

Sunny had occasion to build other houses on his estate, some of which were in Oxford. Often on such matters he was the beneficiary of unsolicited advice from those who lived on the Estate. In 1912 he received a long letter from Mr Stuge who despite signing himself as 'Your Grace's obedient servant' proceeded to tell the Duke exactly what he was doing wrong with the new houses being built for Estate workers in Combe and Hanborough. The crux of the issue was that the houses were being built of brick rather than stone. Mr Stuge felt red brick was out of character and reminded him of his duty 'to preserve all the inherited beauty of his estate.' Sunny's reply is unknown but the houses were built in brick.

There were other building issues that required his attention. Repairs to the local churches of Woodstock and Bladon were a constant drain on his finances. In September 1896 he gave £500 for restoration works at Woodstock Church. In 1902 he spent £68 on Bladon Churchyard. The estate ledgers show that he also helped other local churches, but not to such an extent as he helped Woodstock & Bladon. In 1906 the Vicar of Combe Church, Mr Spencer-Peake, wrote requesting financial help for repair work needed to the church. He sent £20.

Sunny was an Anglican for most of his life, becoming a Catholic in later years. Whether Anglican or Catholic he supported all the churches in the surrounding villages. In 1893 he gave a parcel of land so a chapel could be built in Long Hanborough. The local vicar, the Reverend James Bellamy, had noticed that the numbers attending divine service from Long Hanborough were dwindling because his parishioners had to walk to Church Hanborough each Sunday as there was no church in Long Hanborough. He therefore asked the Duke for land and on 5 April 1893 the deed of gift was signed. Christ Church Chapel was built and it still stands today and is a working church. He also donated the land needed to build the Wesleyan Chapel in Long Hanborough and this church was opened in 1895. As well as supporting the living he helped with the dead. He agreed to sell land to Witney Town Burial Board for a new graveyard.

He gave generously of his time, his pocket and his home to support all kinds of events and good causes. Often this was done by giving access to the Park, Gardens and Palace. Many different groups and associations wrote to him requesting permission to visit the Palace or to hold rallies, picnics and meetings in the Park. The list of requests was endless and it seems most were granted.

The kinds of groups who used the Park were varied in character and at times the numbers visiting were very large. On 7 August 1899 Sunny gave out the prizes at the Temperance Fête which was held in the Park. Being an excellent drinker himself and with friends like Winston Churchill and F.E. Smith who were exceptional participants, it is perhaps amusing to think of the young Duke spending the afternoon in the company of a large group of people who abhorred alcohol. Nevertheless, he did his duty.

In May 1910 Mr Adolphus Ballard wrote asking permission to hold: the 'Methodists' big meeting in Blenheim Park.' The Methodists planned to hold a picnic followed by speeches. Sunny replied that they were allowed to have their meeting on the understanding that 'there should be no allusion to politics!'

He was, all his life, a convinced Conservative and the Conservative Party often visited and on those occasions there was a great deal of allusion to politics. On 17 August 1899 the Conservative Fête was held in the gardens at Blenheim. Sunny welcomed them with a short speech. His two closest friends and cousins, Winston Churchill and Ivor Guest were also present. There was boating on the lake, roundabouts for the children and tea in the riding school. The Conservatives each paid a small amount towards the cost, which amounted to approximately half the cost of the day and Sunny paid the balance.

Sunny was not always in residence when the various groups and societies visited the Park or held their rallies at Blenheim, but he made a particular effort for the Chelsea Pensioners, fifty of whom visited Blenheim on 5 September 1899 for the day. They marched from Long Hanborough station in their magnificent uniforms and crowds gathered to see them pass. Accompanied by the Duchess, Sunny met them in the Great Hall at the Palace and gave them luncheon in the Arcade Room (Water Terrace Café today). After lunch the pensioners had a stroll in the gardens and then the Duke and Duchess gave them a personal tour of the Palace. The day did not end there. After the tour the pensioners were taken back to the Arcade Room for afternoon tea. They left by the 4:30 p.m. train from Hanborough Station tired but very well fed. The weather had been beautiful all day and Mr Hine noted in his diary that all the pensioners were 'highly pleased with their outing.'

The same courtesy was extended to other visiting groups if Sunny was in residence. In 1925 Mr Goldstone, General Secretary of the National Union of Teachers wrote to thank him for his 'great courtesy' when they visited Blenheim in May:

The members greatly appreciated the personal interest you took in them, and the pleasure of their stay was greatly enhanced by the opportunities which were provided for inspecting your historic mansion.

Perhaps the most unusual event which took place in the Park happened on 16 August 1900 when a tightrope walker walked across the lake on his tightrope for the entertainment of the foresters who had gathered for their fête in the Park. Foresters came from all over the country for this fête, which was held annually in Blenheim Park and it seems they always had some form of special entertainment laid on. In 1899 they had the spectacle of a balloon ascent from the cricket pitch (South Lawn). This was to prove too exciting as the balloon very quickly came down again and lodged in trees, much to the consternation of the Duke and Duchess who were watching along with the foresters. Things went off much more successfully the previous year when the balloonist, Professor Fleet from Oxford, took his balloon up to 14,200 feet then leapt out and parachuted down to the delight of the watching crowds. One assumes he left an assistant in the basket to bring the balloon down.

Sunny gave generous support to the church and church societies, both locally and nationally. In May 1912 the Church of England Waifs and Strays Society had their meeting at Blenheim. Until he left the Anglican faith, the Duke was a fully committed member of the Church. The Living of Bladon and Woodstock was in the gift of the Duke of Marlborough and therefore had his particular attention. When it was necessary to choose a new rector he would seek recommendations, although as soon as it was known that a new incumbent was required the letters flooded in. In February 1895 Lord Edgcumbe wrote to him concerning the Reverend Farmer and recommended him for the Living at Bladon & Woodstock.

> My Dear Sunny
> Mr Farmer held for some years the Living of Millbrook, a village close by here, to which I presented him. Both he and his wife are excellent people.

He went on to say that Farmer was 'self-sacrificing, a gentleman and a moderately high churchman'. On this occasion there were eighteen applicants for the position. The land agent, Mr Angas, made a list with notes and the names of the referees next to each. Mr. Angas felt that the Reverend Farmer was most suited to the post. He was duly appointed and remained in post until 1905.

Whilst the schools in all the surrounding villages were church schools, a considerable amount of financial support for each school came from the Estate. In one of the Estate Ledgers the Duke is shown to have given money to twenty schools. In 1902 the Estate Ledger records that Bladon School alone cost him £212.13s.7d. The Estate helped with all sorts of expenses. In August 1909 Mr Everitt, the deputy land agent, arranged to have the local builder, Mr Tolley from Bladon, clear out the school toilets. Mr Tolley wrote to Everitt saying: 'I should like to do the WCs tonight as the wind is the right way to blow the stench from the village.' It was lucky for the village of Bladon that the builder was so thoughtful! In August 1912 Sunny paid to have the drains overhauled at Bladon School.

Every summer and every Christmas the Duke and Duchess gave a 'treat' to the local school children. They were all invited to the Palace for afternoon tea, games, fair rides and a Punch and Judy show. Each child left with a piece of fruit and a cake or a bag of sweets. It was not just the Woodstock and Bladon children who were invited to these jamborees, the children of Old Woodstock, Wootton, Stonesfield and Hempton also attended. On 22 August 1901 there were 750 children at the 'treat' and Mr Hine wrote in his diary:

> The children assembled about 2:15 [p.m.] and were met by Her Grace on the steps at the South Front. Tea was served on long tables in front of the Arcade Rooms. There were Roundabouts, Swings, Cocoa Nut shies, and a Punch and Judy show … also a string band. Before tea the children had some races and after tea Her Grace presented each child with a toy and a bag of sweets. The weather was beautiful and everything passed of [sic] most successfully.

Another year, when the weather was inclement the tea was held in the Indoor Horse Arena and both Sunny and Consuelo helped to serve the children.

Blenheim Park was a favoured destination for Sunday School outings. Each year many different churches in Oxford and the surrounding villages brought their Sunday Schools to the Park for a treat. Some came by train and some by horse drawn charabanc. Those from nearby village churches walked. In July 1909 St Thomas Church, Oxford brought their

The south lawn was often used for picnics and treats, as well as being the location of the cricket pitch, during the season, as it is today.

Sunday School children to the Park for their summer treat and tea as did Marston Street Church and St John the Evangelist Church in Oxford. Clearly the Duke's gardeners and gate staff had a busy time in July dealing with excitable children.

Sunny made sure there was an annual 'treat' not just for the children but also for his tenants. He had a stern but paternalistic attitude towards his many tenants. Some of his tenants were overseeing large farms and others rented a small cottage and allotment. Whatever their status or holding he was always concerned for their welfare. Whilst the Duchess sent food and sympathy when someone was ill, the Duke sent practical help like free hospital bed letters. There would always be a summer fête and a Christmas present for his tenants. On 14 June 1897 Sunny and Consuelo held a garden party for their tenants and the Oxfordshire Yeomanry. There were approximately 200 guests. They arrived at 2:00 p.m. and were greeted in person in the Long Library. Mr Perkins played the Willis Organ for the assembled company. The guests were also entertained by Mr Priestley's Band and a Miss Bartlett, who presumably sang. There was also music outside and the Titcombe Band played down near the boathouse for the people going boating on the lake and exploring the gardens. The guests were given refreshments in the Arcade Rooms.

It was these kinds of annual events which bound Sunny and his family to the local people, and for which he was held in high esteem. It was the natural order of society at that time to revere the nobility but the people who lived and worked on the Estate, learned that whilst he was a serious and at times difficult man, he was also generous and caring. It was not surprising then that there was consternation but also a certain amount of pride when the Duke volunteered for active duty in South Africa sailing from Southampton on 22 January 1900. When he left he took with him the good wishes of the whole of Woodstock and all those on his estate. It was a serious concern for the local people to have their Duke going off to fight. Their livelihoods depended on him and his heir was still only a child. The local dignitaries in Woodstock were proud to mark the Duke's departure to the war and their 'address' was reported in full in the local newspaper, *Jackson's Oxford Journal* on 6 January 1900:

> At a meeting of the Committee of Tenantry on the Marlborough Estates, held at the Marlborough Arms, Woodstock, on Tuesday, Mr Thomas Smith, presiding, the appended address to His Grace was approved. It had been intended that the address should be engrossed and illuminated, but the Duke suggested that the money that would be thus spent should be given to the War Relief Fund, and that any address that they might wish to present to him should be merely plainly written or printed.

The address, which had therefore been printed in the circular form, reads as follows:

To the Most Nobel [Sic] Charles Richard John, Duke of Marlborough

My Lord Duke, – May it please Your Grace, we, the whole of the tenants on the Blenheim Estates, learn that owing to the grave state of affairs at the seat of War in South Africa and the danger thereby occasion to the safety of the Empire, Your Grace has volunteered to proceed at once to take part in the arduous and trying duties of a warrior's life, and to help to defend the honour and integrity of the Empire against the aggression of no mean foe.

We, Your Grace's tenants, cannot allow such an heroic act of duty and self-denial as this to pass unnoticed, much as we regret the danger to which Your Grace's person will be exposed thereby; we therefore beg Your Grace to accept our admiration of the courage and valour Your Grace here displays, which is worthy of our most illustrious ancestor, the First Duke of Marlborough. We therefore beg the acceptance of this short and unpretentious address as a medium of conveying to Your Grace and Her Grace, the Duchess, our devotion to your person for the enormous self-sacrifice made by this voluntary call to serve your Queen and Country and obey a call to duty. Such an example must have a very beneficial effect on all those who are wavering, and act as an incentive to those who have already volunteered.

We pray that God... May shortly restore you in health and crowned with laurels to your charming home and family.

Signed on behalf of the Tenantry

Thomas Smith, Chairman

R.R. Pratt, Secretary

These sentiments were shared by people of all stations in life beyond Woodstock where Sunny's Estate extended because he was a good landlord and always took his responsibilities to those who lived and worked on his land very seriously. He thanked them for their kind thoughts.

On 14 February 1900 the Oxfordshire County Council held their Quarterly meeting. They decided to place on record their:

High appreciation of the sense of patriotism and the sacrifice of personal interests which had actuated their Chairman (Viscount Valentia M.P.) and the Duke of Marlborough (another member of their body), in engaging themselves for active service in S. Africa.

Sunny was not present to receive these commendatory remarks and neither was Viscount Valentia; both were already on their way to South Africa.

Sunny served in the South African War with the Imperial Yeomanry and he was mentioned in dispatches in 1900. The people of Woodstock

The Duke ready for military service in South Africa, in the uniform of a staff officer.

and the Blenheim Estate were very relieved when he returned, alive and well from the war. Once again they gathered to mark the occasion and the celebrations were reported in *The Times* on 2 August 1900:

> The Duke of Marlborough, who reached England from South Africa on Friday, met with an enthusiastic reception on his return to Blenheim Palace last evening. He was accompanied by the Duchess. They were met at Woodstock Station by the Mayor and Corporation, who presented the Duke with an address congratulating him upon his safe return and welcoming him back to the home of his ancestors.
>
> The Duke and Duchess drove to the Park amid great enthusiasm, and upon the steps of the grand entrance further addresses were presented to His Grace by Mr T Smith, of Campsfield, on behalf of the Tenantry, and by Mr Angas, Estate Steward, on behalf of the employees. The Duke, in reply, in referring to his experiences in South Africa, said the Regular troops expressed the greatest admiration at the way in which the Imperial Yeomanry conducted themselves in the field. Speaking for himself, he

could say he had brought back an extraordinary store of good health and
a bag full of Kruger sovereigns.

Three hearty cheers were given for the Duke and Duchess at the conclusion of the proceedings.

Consuelo and Ivor, by Giovanni Boldini, 1906

4

Ducal responsibilities

As head of a substantial estate the 9th Duke received a continual flow of requests for help and money from all sorts of people. These claims on his finances were many and varied. They were sometimes sent direct and at other times came via his land agent. The land agent had the authority to deal with certain requests himself but often the letters he received were forwarded to the Duke. Sunny would make a note in pencil in the top left hand corner of the letter stating what was to be done or the amount given. What becomes clear from the many, many letters is that everyone who asked for help was given help. Sometimes this was in the form of money and sometimes it was more practical as when he gave a joint of beef to the Stonesfield Benefit Society Annual dinner. Occasionally it was a matter of giving tenants time to pay their rent.

In 1909 Emily Timms (the Timms family lived on the Estate for several generations and several Timms men were gardeners for successive Dukes) wrote to the land agent from her rented home, Rose Cottage in Bladon:

> Sir
>
> I humbly beg your pardon writing to you, I received your letter from the office about my rent, I should have sent it up, but I was waiting for my daughter to send it from London. As soon as I hear from her I will send [it] up. My rent has always been paid ever since His Grace allowed me to remain in the old home after my Mother's death, widow Long, you may not remember her. (He did remember. There were many Longs working

as Gamekeepers for the Duke). We have rented the home 60 years last month. ... I hope I shall be able to pay it this week.

I humbly beg your pardon.

I remain your humble and obedient servant

Emily Timms

The Duke wrote on the letter: 'Give time'.

On other occasions it was a case of allowing tenants to pay less. In 1895, before his marriage to Consuelo Vanderbilt brought in a considerable injection of cash, the Estate was running at a loss. That year the harvest was poor and some of the tenant farmers were facing difficulties. The Duke gave instructions that, across the Estate, he would accept less rent.

Sunny made financial contributions to all kinds of local associations that were set up to help the poor. He donated to poor funds and in particular to Pig Funds. Most of the local villages had Pig Funds. Charitable donors would buy a pig and pay for its upkeep. It was then slaughtered for the benefit of the poor in the village. In 1912, for example, Mr Savill from the Bladon Benefit Pig Fund wrote to the land agent:-

The committee of the Bladon Benefit Pig Fund wish me to offer their best thanks to His Grace for kindly subscribing to their funds last year. They hope he will grant them the same favour this year.

The Duke did, however it was Mr Palmer, the then land agent, who was invited to the Pig Club's dinner organised to thank all the subscribers. That year he also sent money to the Combe Poor Fund & the Almswomen Fund in Woodstock.

In June 1912 the Salvation Army in Stonesfield found that they were £8 in debt. Captain Ryan wrote to the Duke and explained that the expenses had been higher than usual as so many people were in want because of the lack of work and the coal strike. Captain Ryan said: 'I am writing to you in the hope that you will help us a little financially...for which I should be very grateful.' He was not a man to wait and finished by saying: 'I shall call on Wednesday morning for an answer to this letter by 11am.'

Easing the suffering of individuals

Sunny also received numerous requests for money from people who found themselves in difficult circumstances. These requests were always dealt with favourably, even for people who did not live on the Duke's land or work for him. In March 1912 he received a letter from Mr J. Shagles who was a labourer living in Charlbury and not in his employ. Mr Shagles wanted to emigrate to Canada but could not afford to do so and because he was not an agricultural labourer he could not get 'the usual help from the government in regard to passage.' The Duke told the land agent to send 10 shillings. It cost approximately £10 to buy passage to Canada at the time so Mr Shagles still needed a lot more, but it was a start. Sunny had a very typical Victorian attitude towards charity. He would help and he did help, but he also expected people to work and help themselves. In the early 1900s enormous numbers of people emigrated to Canada. In December 1907 *The Times* reported that a quarter of million were expected to settle in Canada in 1908.

Sunny's first wife, Consuelo, was well known locally for her charitable work and in particular for providing funds to give work to local unemployed men to rebuild the Estate roads. He, whilst less well known for adopting this, agreed with the principle. In 1909 a new well had to be dug at Eagle Lodge. The Duke instructed it was to be dug using men 'out of employment' rather than those already employed by the Estate.

Requests for money followed him wherever he went. On 21 June 1909, whilst in London, Sunny received a long letter from a former servant, Charles Turrell, who had fallen on hard times because of ill health. In the letter Mr Turrell reminded the Duke that he had always been kind and generous towards his family, 'and the last of Your Grace's many acts of kindness to us [was] giving my sister one of the alms-houses.' (In which it is clear that Mr Turrell was also living). Mr Turrell had started at Blenheim as a Steward's Room Boy and rose to be a Footman with the 7th Duke. He had travelled to Ireland with the family when the 7th Duke was made Lord Lieutenant of Ireland. He continued in his letter to say:

> I could mention many happy incidents when I used to be sent out on the lawn to bowl to Your Grace, then Earl of Sunderland, for a game of cricket at the Viceregal Lodge.

Mr Turrell received £1.

During Sunny's lifetime there were of course great strides made in social reform with a raft of Parliamentary Acts brought in by the Liberal Government in the early 1900s. The Duke was not universally in favour of these reforms and made his opposition clear in the House of Lords. It was not that he objected to helping those with difficulties, because he did this throughout his life. He objected to having to pay more taxes for these reforms because he was already giving financial assistance to large numbers of needy people whether they lived on his Estate or not; what he objected to was paying twice.

He was a safety net for those who were bold enough to ask for help even if they did not live anywhere near his lands and for those who lived on his Estate. In 1910 Harriet Albury wrote to him asking for financial help. She was a widow aged sixty-eight who made her living by taking in lodgers and making gloves (something for which Woodstock was famous). She said in her letter: 'My last lodger left me 3 weeks back to get married. Since then I have had nothing to depend on which has brought me to want.' The Duke sent her 10 shillings.

Medical requests

In the late 1800s and early 1900s it was a very expensive business to be ill and Sunny received numerous requests for help with medical problems, medical bills and 'Free Bed Letters'. On 12 September 1910 Norah Wilson wrote thanking him for his help:

> I write to thank Your Grace for your kindness in paying my expenses to St. John's Brine Bath Hospital, Droitwich on 11th August. I feel sure Your Grace will be pleased to hear I received great benefit from the Baths.

In February 1909 George Vitler wrote requesting a 'Free Bed Letter' for his two year old son who had 'deformed feet.' Mr Vitler worked for the S.E.&C. Railway and earned £1 a week. He was not a local man but the Duke had a 'Free Bed Letter' sent to him.

Sunny was not the first Marlborough to help with matters medical. He inherited the duty to help others with medical costs from his forebears and he took this responsibility very seriously. After the 7th Duke of Marlborough died in 1883 the Marlborough Memorial Fund was established and managed by a Committee. Its funds were invested and the income this generated was given to the Radcliffe Infirmary in Oxford. Sunny was on this Committee and took a close interest in its work. In December 1921 he gave a parcel of land to the Infirmary upon which to build a smallpox hospital.

Blenheim Hospital

During the First World War the Palace itself became a hospital for wounded soldiers. In 1914 Sunny's sisters and Gwendoline Spencer-Churchill (Winston Churchill's sister-in-law) set up a fifty-bed convalescence hospital at the Palace. The main part of the hospital was in the Long Library but there was also a surgery, a reading room and a smoking room for the wounded soldiers.

This hospital was run by the most impressive Sister A. Munn and she was helped by a small team of nurses, one of whom was her sister, Nurse M. Munn. The Woodstock local doctor and chemist attended patients regularly. Mrs Rimand (the Duke's housekeeper) arranged for the soldiers' washing to be done in the Palace laundry and the ladies of the parish knitted bed jackets for each man. The first wounded to arrive at Blenheim were Belgian soldiers and they were followed by English soldiers who came from all over the country, as far north as Newcastle and near at hand, Oxford. These men had a variety of wounds and the length of their stay varied according to the severity of their injuries. The most common injury was gunshot wounds. Some were shot in the leg, others in the arm, some in the chest, some in the foot or head. There were also soldiers with foot problems, particularly trench foot. One man had appendicitis and another had influenza.

Sister Munn ran the hospital at Blenheim with great compassion and efficiency. She believed that if a man was to recover fully then care had to be taken of his emotional state as well as his physical wounds. Sister Munn understood the importance of fresh air and encouraged the men out into the park and gardens as often as she could. In support of this policy Sunny purchased wicker wheelchairs, fishing rods and a football for the men who could still play. Male nurses from the St. John's Ambulance service did night duty in the hospital.

The Blenheim Hospital was open for approximately fifteen months and after it closed Sister Munn left to be Matron at Roehampton

The convalescence hospital in the Long Library, Christmas 1914.

Auxiliary Hospital and her sister went to work in a field hospital in France. Many of the men who convalesced at the Palace wrote letters of thanks to the Duke and to Sister Munn. They also signed and wrote brief notes of thanks in a book which is now in the Blenheim Library. Overwhelmingly they felt that Blenheim was a peaceful haven after the noise and clamour of the trenches.

Sunny was committed to many associations. Although he favoured local causes he assisted many national causes outside Oxfordshire.

Sister Munn and some of the wounded soldiers convalescing in the Long Library at Blenheim.

Rather surprisingly for such a contained and quiet person he was a supporter of the Actors Benevolent Fund. Less surprisingly he supported many initiatives to help the poor especially with matters to do with health. On 28 February 1899 he presided over the annual meeting of the National Orthopaedic Hospital. Early in May 1899 he attended a meeting to establish a fund to raise money for a new children's hospital in South London. Among those in attendance were the Lord Mayor of London, the Duke of Westminster and the Bishop of Rochester. In June 1899 he attended the annual meeting for the Deptford Fund. This was a project to raise money for a new building in Creek Road London. It was a success and by 9 June 1899 £9,345 had already been raised towards the total cost of £10,732.

The Duke was often commandeered to help other members of the family with their charitable affairs. On 18 November 1899 Lady Randolph and a group of wealthy American ladies organised a fundraising

Sister Munn and some of her patients outside the west front of Blenheim Palace.

event at Claridge's Hotel in London. The purpose of the performance was to raise money for an American hospital ship (for soldiers in South Africa). The actual show was a series of moving pictures showing the Executive of the Hospital at work. Sunny was put in charge of the bar.

All of Sunny's family gave their time for good public causes and this was particularly so during the First World War. At the start of the First World War *The Times* newspaper regularly reported the Duke's movements, remarking on his return from the Front with dispatches or on his departure for the Front. He spent the early years of the war travelling backwards and forwards between London and France. At the same time every male member of his extended family, who was of age, served either in the air, in the trenches or at sea. Five of his cousins were wounded fighting at the Front. Early in the war one cousin died of the effects of exposure in the trenches, one uncle was taken prisoner and another uncle was killed in action. The women on all sides of the family threw themselves into war work, determined to do their bit. Such work served as a distraction from the worry of sons, nephews, husbands and brothers being killed or wounded at the Front.

At this time Consuelo was separated from Sunny, but she was still the Duchess of Marlborough. When war broke out in August 1914 she was in America so she hurried home to Sunderland House in London. She very quickly became engrossed in the war effort and throughout the hostilities raised funds for many different war-related causes, in particular for the Red Cross. She administered the Domestic Servants' Red Cross Fund, which raised enough to purchase an ambulance. Between 26 January and 21 February 1915 this ambulance carried 185 wounded soldiers to safety. The fund also paid for twenty beds at the military hospital in Netley in Hampshire. By the end of March 1915 this fund had raised £1,364.0s.7d.

Consuelo along with Lady Randolph Churchill, was also involved with the American Women's War Relief Fund which raised money for and ran a military hospital in Devon. She believed that women were more than capable of taking on men's work. Consuelo helped run the Women's Emergency Corps which intended to train women to take on the jobs left vacant by the men who went to war. Women took on such jobs as doctors, interpreters, chauffeurs, motor-cyclists, gardeners, omnibus conductors, omnibus and taxi-cab drivers.

Consuelo appreciated that the men at the Front needed some light relief from the realities of trench life. In December 1916 she organised a concert at the Palace Theatre in London, which was known as the 'American Matinee' to raise funds to pay for concerts for soldiers at the Front. The concert was a great success.

Of all the ladies in the family it was however Lady Sarah Wilson who worked the hardest and achieved the most. Lady Sarah Wilson (one of Sunny's aunts) raised an enormous amount of money and organised the building of several Red Cross Hospitals in France and Belgium along with a convalescence home in England. She was a woman of great determination and character. An indefatigable woman, her first appeal for funds for a hospital was published in *The Times* within days of the declaration of war. By October 1914 the Chief Surgeon, Mr Oliver Williams, was on his way to Boulogne with thirty-three nurses, where Lady Sarah awaited them. Lady Sarah had arranged for Harrods to not only equip the hospital but also to undertake the catering, so the wounded soldiers

Lady Sarah Wilson, in the dark dress, one of Sunny's formidable aunts.

had the very best of everything. The Duchess of Roxburghe donated £500 to the first of Lady Sarah Wilson's hospitals. She was also President of the Hospital Committee and Earl Howe (Lady Sarah Wilson's brother-in-law) was the Treasurer. The hospital was very much a family affair.

Shortly after the hospital was opened Lady Sarah received the news that her husband, Lieutenant Colonel Gordon Wilson had been killed in action on 6 November 1914. If anything the loss of her husband spurred her on to work even harder. Rather daringly she also sold lingerie at a shop in Piccadilly to raise funds for the Women's Army Auxiliary Corps. In this she was helped by Lady Randolph Churchill and Mrs F.E. Smith (wife of Sunny's great friend, the future Lord Birkenhead). Along with Lady Randolph, Lady Sarah also raised money for free buffets at British railway stations for soldiers and sailors. Assisting the war effort in France she raised money for and worked in soldiers canteens. At this time, when aristocratic ladies were usually protected from the realities of war, Lady Sarah's work left her in no doubt of its horrors. She was an exceptional lady.

The last person in the family to be killed in the war was not one of the many men fighting at the Front. It was a woman. Lady Alexandra Phyllis Hamilton, Sunny's cousin, along with her two servants, Martha Bridge and Ellenor Strachan. They were on board the Irish steamer, R.M.S. (Royal Mail Steamer) Leinster when it was attacked by the German submarine UB-123 on 10 October 1918. The ship was en route from Kingstown to Holyhead when it was hit by two torpedoes just outside Dublin Bay. Over five hundred people were killed when the ship went down. Lady Phyllis' family were told by a survivor that as the ship sank Phyllis gave her life jacket to one of the servants, saying: 'I'm a strong swimmer.' In a report by one of the survivors, Second Lieutenant Hugh Parker, Military Adjutant of the R.M.S. Leinster, he remembered Lady Phyllis in particular for her calm, cheerful and brave demeanour throughout the crisis. In general he thought all the ladies were 'absolutely magnificent'. The family held a memorial service for Lady Phyllis and her two servants on 14 October at St Marks Church in London. Sunny's mother, Albertha who was aunt to Lady Phyllis, and his sisters, Lady Norah Spencer-Churchill and Lady Lilian Grenfell, were amongst the many mourners at the service. The bodies were lost at sea.

Taking care of the servants

The Duke may have at times been a difficult employer but he was also a caring employer to his enormous staff. In addition to the Palace indoor servants there were gardeners, foresters, gamekeepers, watermen, shepherds, cowmen, electricians, gate staff and stable hands to mention a few. Each set of servants was overseen by what would be called a head of department today. At the Palace there were many skilled people working both outside and within.

Sunny expected high standards from all his servants and they all worked long hours, but he was a generous employer and also careful to provide for them at Christmas, Easter and great family occasions. At Christmas there were gifts for the indoor servants and beef or goose for the Estate workers. When he was married in New York in November 1895 the Estate workmen were given a holiday and a feast. For the indoor servants there was dancing afterwards with 'a stage in the Audit Room and a platform in the Riding School'. He did not forget the Gate staff who had to man the gates whilst others attended the dance and he instructed that food and beer was to be taken out to them. The wedding festivities at Blenheim cost £184.6s.5d. This total included paying bell-ringers in the surrounding villages to ring the bells to mark the occasion.

Before the wedding took place the wedding bouquet was prepared in the walled garden using flowers from the Blenheim hothouses. It was packed in ice and sent to Liverpool and from there by ship to New York. So the head gardener and the two Palace florists, who were also garden-ers, played a very important part in the wedding itself.

When the Duke and Duchess returned from their honeymoon they were received with a rapturous welcome from the people of Woodstock, the Estate workers and the Palace servants. In fact Mr Angas, the land agent, and the Town Mayor had set up a committee to organise the 'Welcome'.

Gerald Horne, hall boy, vividly remembered the day the Duke brought Consuelo home to the Palace:

> A day I shall always remember was when the Duke brought his bride – Miss Consuelo Vanderbilt as she had been – back from their honeymoon in Egypt. Woodstock of course was smothered in flags and at the station the Bays were taken from the shafts and the carriage with our master and mistress was drawn by the estate men to the town hall and from there to the palace in triumph. It was a great thing for me to stand there and see them brought home in such style and when the Duchess stepped down from the carriage you might almost have heard us gasp as how young and how beautiful she was. And she was as good as she was beautiful too. In fact she would go out of her way to be kind to everyone and of course she was idolised. At Christmas, for instance, she saw to it personally that everyone in the villages belonging to Blenheim had a blanket or a pig or a ton of coal or whatever it was they wanted. She was a great lady.

As the Duke and his new Duchess led a peripatetic life, significant events such as the birth of an heir could and did happen away from Blenheim. On each occasion Sunny ensured the servants were given a suitable party.

The welcoming committee arranged for Woodstock to be decorated ready for the homecoming of the Duke and his new Duchess.

Gerald Horne remembered the birth of Lord Blandford, John Albert Spencer-Churchill, because of the celebrations that followed:

You can imagine what a day it was when we heard that an heir – Lord Blandford – had been born in London. The steward and his staff at once climbed to the palace roof and fired a salute; and at night a ball was given for the servants and the people of Woodstock and the rest. The menservants wore dress clothes with special buttonholes. I was in my morning suit (but I managed the buttonhole all right; I doubt if any man's was larger) and danced with the maids, who looked very nice and graceful in their own long dresses. (For their daily work in the palace they were given black dresses – the only place I have known where this was done.) We danced to the organ as well as to a string band. All the elaborate refreshments were prepared in the palace kitchens and then passed from hand to hand by a row of waiters reaching from kitchen to dining room. Free beer, free everything flowed like milk and honey. The beer cellar by the way was quite a noted place. We would get in two dozen barrels at a time.

Blenheim protocol

Whenever Sunny came home with his family or with a house party, there was much work for the servants to be done in preparation for their arrival. He would send a brief note or telegram to let Mr Angas know when he and his wife would be arriving at Blenheim and he always gave his housekeeper and butler fair warning of house parties. He would write, usually via the land agent, giving instructions and the names of guests. Sometimes he would say that he expected Mrs Rimand, the housekeeper, to organise who slept where, and at other times he would specify the rooms. In 1906, for example, The Duke wrote to Mr Angas from London:

> Dear Angas
>
> Please give a copy of the enclosed list to both Fletcher (Butler) and Mrs Rimand. Tell the latter to arrange the rooms as she thinks best. I hope you have arranged trains for Saturday. I shall get down early on Saturday morning.
>
> Marlborough

The guest list on that occasion included:

> Viscount and Viscountess Churchill & Miss Taylor
> Mr and Mrs Bonar Law
> Colonel and Lady Sarah Wilson
> Hon. G. Guinness and Lady Evelyn Guinness
> Rt. Hon. W.S. Churchill
> Lord Allendale
> Mr E Marsh (Winston's private Secretary)
> Rt. Hon. Lloyd George
> Sir Ian Hamilton
> Viscount & Viscountess Ridley
> The Earl and Countess of Arran
> Lady N Churchill
> Mr Perkins (Organist)

At the end of the list the Duke added a footnote:

> Please give a copy at once to Mrs Rimand and to Fletcher otherwise they
> will both pretend they know nothing!

Clearly he had not always seen eye to eye with his butler and housekeeper.

Sunny would be described today as a man who liked to micromanage. Perhaps this was a function of his character, perhaps necessity but whatever the reason he was capable of nagging the servants on the smallest of issues. This is particularly apparent in a letter sent to Mr Fletcher in the summer of 1921, when he was on his honeymoon with his second wife, Gladys:

> Mr Fletcher
> Are you getting the money back for empties? This Bill is high. I shall
> move the stores if you cannot be careful.

There was a note in this letter for the housekeeper too:

> These bills must be looked through. Why a grocer as well as the stores.
> Kindly explain. Pray see that economy is practiced [sic] while I am away.
> Marlborough.

It is surprising that he would concern himself with the issue of 'empties' whilst on his honeymoon but he liked to keep the servants on their toes.

Life at the Palace could and often did involve grand occasions for royalty and visiting dignitaries but it could also be quiet and slow of pace. Surprisingly the Duke could and did live very simply when he was not entertaining and in particular after he and Consuelo had gone their separate ways. Writing to Angas from London in May 1908 he informed his land agent:

> Dear Angas
> I am coming to Blenheim on Friday till Monday. The kitchen maid will
> do for me... I hope that the cleaning of the house progresses...
> Will you tell Mrs Rimand that I will sleep upstairs and use the gun
> room not my sitting room.

Having established that he could manage with the minimum attention from the servants it must be said he was writing from the Ritz Hotel in London!

Normally when the Duke was in residence there was a full staff ready to serve him and his guests. There was a strict hierarchy amongst the servants with the butler as the head of the household staff with particular responsibility for the male servants. The housekeeper was next in importance and she oversaw all the female staff. When visitors came to stay they did of course bring their own servants who then had to be slotted into this hierarchy of the servants hall. Their status depended on the status of their master or mistress. A Countess ranked lower than a Duchess and the servants of an 'Honourable' were even lower in the pecking order. Royal servants took precedence over the Duke's servants. The visiting servants were not only fed but also had to be accommodated and not everyone enjoyed sharing. Gerald Horne remembered in his memoirs when the Prince of Wales came to stay at Blenheim:

> Naturally the Duke and Duchess entertained very lavishly. Wonderful week-end parties they gave, with tea in the boathouse and the Blue Hungarian Band from London to play at dinner, not to mention Mr. Perkins' organ playing afterwards. But the greatest occasion of all during my time at Blenheim was the visit of the late King Edward, then Prince of Wales, and the Princess. The Princess Victoria was also of the party, as were Prince and Princess Charles of Denmark and they all stayed several days for the shooting. There were thirty-six guests and on the evening of their arrival we had first a torchlight procession (and very pretty it looked crossing the Lake by the old stone bridge) and then a banquet. Well some of us were given permission to go up on the balcony that night and look down and there it was, all gleaming with wealth. I think the first thing that struck me was the flashing headgears of the ladies. The Blue Hungarian was playing and there was the Prince himself looking really royal and magnificent in military uniform. The table was laid of course with the silver gilt service, and the royal footmen waiting side by side with our own.

When Sunny was not in residence for a long period of time the Palace servants were put on 'Board Wages' which meant they were paid less because they had less to do. When in residence the Duke did pay well and gave generous annuities to those who retired from his service. He may have been exacting in the standards he expected and certainly was at times a very trying master but it was considered a good job to work for him at Blenheim.

Gerald Horne who was a hall boy for the 9th Duke also had the job of looking after the telephone exchange. He wrote in his memoirs:

> When I found I was in charge of 3 lines connecting the Duke with his estate, I was more than a little nervous. The Duke was all right but he could certainly make one tremble and when he came round with the steward on his monthly inspection you'd most likely hear a roar and think that what was coming down the passage was a giant. Besides seeing to the telephone I was Hall Boy, which meant looking after the under-servants' hall, laying their meals and so on. My pay was £12 a year and two suits of morning clothes made of the pepper and salt stuff which nearly all servants at that time had to wear. My hours were 7 till 11, most of the time on the go, with two afternoons and two evenings off a week.

The Palace was run very efficiently but there were of course occasional problems, sometimes of a personal nature. These were generally dealt with by either the butler or housekeeper or if of a more serious nature by the land agent. If the problem was very serious then the Duke was consulted. On 2 March 1895 Mr Angas wrote on a delicate matter:

> Your Grace
>
> I am sorry to say that the Still Room Maid, lately the Under House-maid, has had to leave here as she has got into trouble with some man and her mother tells me she is to be confined in June.
>
> This is a most unfortunate occurrence, more so as the girl's mother is a widow, a Mrs Cooper, and very badly off. The girl, Annie Cooper, says the man who did the mischief is Smith, a young fellow at the gardens who decorates the Palace with flowers and she says positively that she has had nothing to do with any other man at all, her mother seems to think her story correct. I have interviewed Smith, who swears he has had no connection with the girl whatever. The girl says he promised faithfully to marry her and the man says he never did such a thing. The girl has no

proof she says beyond her own word.

I think the best thing will be to get the girl away when the time arrives to one of the lying in hospitals in London, as it is quite clear the mother cannot afford to keep her. I believe there are some institutions for such fallen girls afterwards, if so it would be a good thing if she could be sent to such a refuge, otherwise her mother will, I'm afraid, not be able to keep her until she can go out again. I am writing this from home as I did not wish to place such unfortunate information in the office letter book.

I remain Your Grace's obedient servant

R. L. Angas

Dealing with the land agent

Sunny's most important employee and the man with the greatest responsibilities was his land agent. Up until 1909 the role was filled by Mr R. L. Angas. Their letters show that they knew each other well and Mr Angas was not afraid to challenge the Duke. Sunny at times was, in return, a very difficult master, particularly over matters of finance. Having inherited an estate in dire financial straits he spent the rest of his life trying to reduce costs, even after his marriage to Consuelo in November 1895. This marriage brought with it a large injection of funds but managing the Estate, principally made up of farms and forestry, was a constant drain on his finances. Judging by Mr Angas' letter of 26 February 1909, it was still running at a loss in the early 1900s.

Your Grace

I have been thinking over seriously what you said Saturday last and this coupled with your letter of the 25th just received has compelled me to come to the decision that it is no use attempting to continue here as Agent.

You said that in your opinion I was spending £1,000 a year unnecessarily through bad administration, and I reflect that you left a written statement in the office for me criticising my management. This is my twentieth year at Blenheim and I have suffered severely from the strain in attempting to run the whole thing satisfactorily, and I cannot see the least chance of being able to reduce your estimated loss to a point which would give you satisfaction.

I ask you therefore to accept this letter as notice that I shall resign my post as agent at Blenheim on 27th August next.

I remain Your Grace's obedient servant

R. L. Angas

Sunny accepted Mr Angas' resignation and replaced him with Mr Palmer. Mr Everitt remained as the Deputy Agent and Mr Josiah Hine remained as the Estate Clerk. Mr Palmer did not last as long as Mr Angas and was replaced by Mr Cecil Argles in May 1917.

Domestic affairs

With the arrival of their two sons Sunny and Consuelo added another set of servants including a nanny and maids and a footman for the nursery. The Duke recorded the arrival of each son in the Palace visitor book at Blenheim.

John Albert Edward Spencer Churchill arrived at 3am on 18th September 1897.

Ivor Spencer Churchill arrived at 3pm on 14th October 1898.

Sunny's first wife, Consuelo, felt that her husband was too lax in terms of discipline with the boys and as a consequence they were not always the best-behaved children. She said in *The Glitter and the Gold* that Blandford (as Albert was always called) grew up 'audacious and wilful', whilst Ivor was 'gentle and sensitive'. Consuelo confessed herself often at a loss at what to do with her wilful older son but whilst she:

> Had definite ideas concerning discipline, [she] had difficulty in overcoming Marlborough's stubborn opposition to any form of punishment. Claiming that he had been bullied by his father (and he had) he refused to exert any control, and punishments became for me a doubly painful duty in view of his critical disapproval.

The Duke was more than capable of disciplining his sons and he did do so, as Eleanor Smith (daughter of F.E. Smith) remembered all too well. She wrote in her memoirs that Christmas was always a wonderful time for the children at Blenheim. She remembered that there were 'flocks' of children and despite the presence of governesses and nannies aplenty, Christmas was a time of almost 'unbridled license'. Eleanor and the younger children were in awe of Blandford and Ivor and looked up to them 'like Gods'. On one occasion, led by Blandford, the children pelted the governesses and nannies with scones and cakes. Sunny was irate and sent Blandford and Ivor to bed without supper.

A time when the servants had to work extra hard was when the Duke entertained on a grand scale. One of the great social engagements of the year in Oxfordshire was the Queen's Own Oxfordshire Hussars (Q.O.O.H.) Ball at the Palace. Sunny was a soldier all his life, albeit for the most part, like Winston, he was as a part time soldier. He was a member of the Q.O.O.H. along with his cousins Winston and Jack Churchill. The Q.O.O.H. (also known as the Oxfordshire Yeomanry) came to Blenheim Park to hold rallies and camps. He supported the Q.O.O.H. regiment in less obvious ways by paying for prizes and contributing to regimental funds. Only on one occasion did the Regimental Sergeant Major (R.S.M.) have to remind the Duke of his expected generosity. On 13 January 1906 the Estate Office received a letter from R.S.M. Goldie of the Q.O.O.H. asking Mr Hine, the Estate Clerk, if he could say when the money for the Regimental Funds and Musketry prizes would arrive from His Grace. It was sent shortly after the letter was received.

The highlight of the social calendar was the Hussars' Ball in the Long Library. All the officers and men wore their dress uniforms, which were particularly spectacular. Sunny enjoyed dancing and he took every opportunity to dance at balls to which he was invited and at balls at which he was the host. One of the most spectacular balls given at the Palace during his lifetime was his coming of age ball, which took place shortly after he became Duke, in 1892. The National Press reported the event in detail. The following is from *Jackson's Oxford Journal*.

> The Duke of Marlborough's Majority Ball at Blenheim
>
> Blenheim has during the week been the scene of rejoicing connected with the coming of age of the Duke of Marlborough, culminating on Friday night in a County Ball at the Palace, for which about five hundred invitations were issued. The guests were received by the Duke and the Marchioness Blandford in the Grand Saloon, passing thence through the State Rooms. ....
>
> All the ladies wore ball gowns and tiaras, and many men wore 'pink' – a truly brilliant and memorable scene. ... [The] dancing was in the Great Library.

In his later years such scenes did not take place at Blenheim. This was not because of a lack of funds but mainly because of a lack of will. He still cared enormously for his estate and all who lived and worked for him, but after two failed marriages his heart had rather lost the will for great house parties and balls in the Long Library. His later years never saw the large numbers of servants and guests gathered under the Blenheim roof as had been the case previously when on one occasion Consuelo recorded there being over one hundred people staying in the Palace.

Blenheim Fire Brigade

One group of servants that Sunny considered absolutely vital were the men who served in the Blenheim Fire Brigade. In all matters to do with life and work on the Estate Sunny paid infuriatingly close attention to detail. Apart from the weather and its consequent effect on the productivity of the Estate's tenant farms the next matter uppermost in his mind was that of fire, particularly the prevention of fire and the fighting of fire. There had been a serious fire at the Palace during the time of the 7th Duke, in 1861. The fire started in the Palace bakery in the East Courtyard and spread quickly, completely destroying the Gallery above the bakery which contained a fine collection of Titian paintings. It was no surprise then that Sunny kept the Blenheim Fire Brigade equipped and ready.

The men who served in the Blenheim Brigade were all servants of the Duke. To cope with any fire Blenheim had fire buckets, stirrup pumps, dry risers in the Palace and a rather splendid steam powered fire engine. The fire engine had been purchased by the 8th Duke in 1888 from Messrs. Merryweather and Sons. Horses pulled the engine and Sunny liked to make sure that they were equal to the task and that everyone knew where they would be when needed. In December 1921 he wrote to Mr Fitzroy saying:

> Kindly report to me where the most suitable horses are for going in the fire engine in the event of fire. When this is determined a notice should be put up at the Fire Engine Station. … it is to be understood that horses are only to go slowly and not to gallop. Marlborough

The last instruction is somewhat surprising, as with such a precious collection in the Palace, one would imagine that he would hope for a respectable turn of speed from his horses. Interestingly Mr Fitzroy replied that mules would be:

> the most suitable animals to pull the fire engine in case of emergency. They will go faster than your farm horses on the level or downhill and will be no slower than horses uphill.

Despite all the precautions there were several fires at the Palace during the Duke's lifetime. One particularly dangerous fire happened shortly after a visit from the Prince of Wales. A serious fire broke out in the roof of the Palace. Gerald Horne, hall boy at the time, thoroughly enjoyed the whole crisis:

> When the royal visit came to an end, as you can imagine, everyone was more or less exhausted, so the Duke and Duchess decided to go away and give us all a complete rest. They had been gone only one day when fire broke out in the roof of the saloon. Luckily the palace fire brigade had been training that morning and had only just left for their quarters. One of the decorators came running to me and calling 'Johnny, there's a fire!

The Blenheim Fire Brigade.

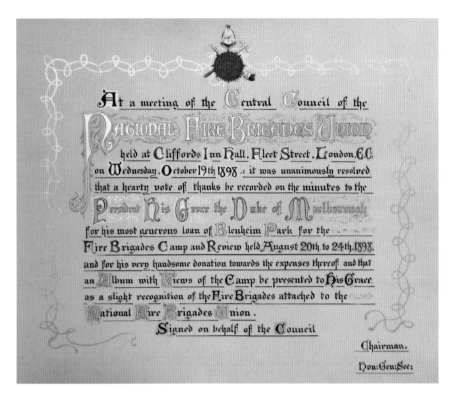

The Frontispiece of the photograph album presented to Sunny in 1898.

Ring the bell!' You bet I tugged with a will and within five minutes the brigade was at the front door and pumping away with their old steamer and manual to the tune of 60,000 gallons an hour.

The thing that tickled me at the time was the panic of the housekeeper. I can see her now as she rushes into the front hall and throwing her arms round a statue that must have weighed five hundred weight if it weighed a pound tries to carry it off. The steward too was in a dither and took a knife to cut down the dining-room tapestries. The land steward came in though before he could do much and stopped him. Everything movable was cleared from the saloon and put on the lawn. The fire had started from a beam in the chimney which must have been smouldering all the time the royal party was with us.

But I shall always remember the part I played in the fire. I don't mean ringing the bell, though that was jolly enough. No, I mean sweeping the

*One of the early photos in the album is a formal one of the Duke and the
Officers representing each Brigade from around the country, sitting outside
the south front of the Palace. Sunny looks very young and serious seated in
the middle of these uniformed men.*

water downstairs when the fire was out. Along came the water, you see,
like a great dirty river to where me and Mike the black page was standing with our brooms at the top of the basement stairs. As you can guess,
nothing gave us more enjoyment than getting our feet into plenty of water
and for nearly an hour that day we both had the time of our lives, yelling
in English and in what I suppose was Egyptian as with all our strength
and enthusiasm we helped the water downstairs.

The fire had done little damage, the water a great deal. The brigade
stayed on and I had to get them food and beer. Still they stayed enjoying
themselves no end, till it all turned into a singsong right up to midnight and
everyone went to bed at least thoroughly happy. What's more the insurance
company sent us all a reward, the firemen a fiver each, our men a pound
and myself fifteen shillings – a tremendous sum to me in those days.

Not too surprisingly Sunny supported the National Fire Brigade Union all
his life and in his younger years he was President of the Union. Between

20 and 24 August 1898 Fire Brigades from all over the country assembled in the Park for several days of parades, displays and competitions.

As a gift of thanks for allowing the rally to take place in the Park at Blenheim the National Fire Brigade Union gave him a photograph album containing pictures of this event. The photos are a detailed record of all the parades, demonstrations and competitions which took place over the five days. Adorning the first page of this enormous, red, leather bound album is a magnificent frontispiece which is beautifully illuminated and says:

Fire Brigade Rally
20th August – 24th August 1898
Blenheim Park
A meeting of the Central Council of the National Fire Brigade Union held at Clifford Inn Hall, Fleet Street, London, EC, on Wednesday October 19th 1898: it was unanimously resolved that a hearty note of thanks be recorded on the minutes to the President, His Grace the Duke of Marlborough for his most generous loan of Blenheim Park for the Fire Brigades Camp and Review held August 20th – 24th 1898 and for his very handsome donation towards the expenses thereof and that an Album of the views of the Camp to be presented to His Grace as a slight recognition of the Fire Brigades attached to the National Fire Brigade union.

One of the early photos in the album is a formal one of the Duke and the Officers representing each Brigade from around the country sitting outside the north front of the Palace. Sunny looks very young and serious seated in the middle of these uniformed men. As part of the event Sunny inspected the firemen with all the brigades lined up in military order and he presented the prizes. The photographs record that the Ilford Fire Brigade won the 'Escape Shield' and the Leyton Brigade won the 'Steamer Shield'. The 'Manual Shield' was won by Bournemouth Fire Brigade. All the horses and equipment were immaculately turned out. Sadly the Blenheim Brigade, led by Captain Scroggs, did not win a prize. Up until quite recently there was still a member of the Scroggs family working at the Palace and of course the Palace still has its own firemen. Their skills could easily match those of the 1898 Brigade but the present day uniform is nowhere near as magnificent as those worn in the time of the 9th Duke.

The various Fire Brigades slept in tents set up in the park during the 1898 Rally. There were also tents for serving food and a set of tents where the camp servants slept.

Blenheim employees and the First World War

On the outbreak of the First World War, many of the men who served in the Blenheim Fire Brigade, along with others from the Estate immediately volunteered for active duty. Many served with the Queen's Own Oxfordshire Hussars and others with the Oxfordshire and Buckinghamshire Light Infantry. In April 1915, the Bladon & Woodstock Parish Magazine recorded that there were 153 men from Bladon & Woodstock on active service in the army including one with the Army Vet Corps and one with the Flying Corps, nine in the Royal Navy and 14 with the Red Cross. The War Memorials in Woodstock and the surrounding villages record the terrible losses faced by families in this area. These Memorials list 'Blenheim names'; the names of men who belonged to families who worked for Sunny and as such were part of the extended Blenheim family. Some of these families worked on the Estate for many generations such as the Hicks, Timms, Rouse, Hine, Long, Danbury, Franklin, Berry, Woodward, Maisey, Margetts, Scroggs, Farley and Hollis.[1]

Thankfully there were times of celebrations as well as grief during the war. This was particularly so for local hero George Woodford, one

The Duke inspecting the massed ranks of firemen at the 1898 Rally
in Blenheim Park.

of Sunny's tenants. Captain Woodford served throughout the war with
the Q.O.O.H and was awarded the Military Cross by King George V at
Buckingham Palace. The citation for his M.C. was:

> Captain George W. Woodford
> Military Distinction
> 'For conspicuous gallantry and devotion to duty during lengthy opera-
> tions. As transport officer he continually brought up rations, water, and
> ammunition under the heaviest fire and most adverse weather conditions.
> His coolness and determination were very marked, and inspired all his
> men to further efforts.'

Before the war, George's father was one of Sunny's tenant farmers who
worked Manor Farm at Kidlington. George himself also became a farmer
working University Farm near Carterton. His brother Frederick was an
electrician at the Palace. As a member of the Q.O.O.H, George knew
Winston Churchill and his brother Jack. George, in full dress uniform,
attended Jack's wedding to Lady Gwendoline Bertie in 1908. In 1911 he

married Christina McDuff, who was head dairymaid at Blenheim. After the war he returned to farming and during the Second World War was a member of the Woodstock Home Guard.

Another local man and servant of the Duke who made the news during the war, was Arthur Hine. Before the war he worked as a clerk in the Blenheim Estate Office with his father Josiah Hine, who was the Estate Clerk. Arthur's grandfather J.E. Hine had also been the estate clerk in his time. Arthur went to war as a member of Q.O.O.H. On the orders of Winston Churchill, in October 1914, men from the Naval Division and men from the Q.O.O.H, including Sergeant Hine were sent to hold back the German advance on Antwerp. This proved impossible and on 8 October the order was given to evacuate the city. Sergeant Hine, who was serving as a dispatch rider, was sent with dispatches to the coast. As he was riding through the city he found a toddler, a Belgian girl, outside her blazing home. There was no one else alive and he knew he could not leave her in such danger so he took her to Calais on the carrier of his motorcycle. They arrived at Calais and he was then ordered to take the dispatches to London. There was nothing to be done other than to take the child with him so he took her to London and from there to his family in Woodstock, who looked after her. Her story after the war is, as yet, unknown.

The war affected and changed the lives of many who lived and worked on the Estate and it certainly affected Sunny and his family. A quick look through the estate ledgers, however, shows that in many ways life at Blenheim went on as normal during and after the war had ended. The Duke was a traditional man and during the war, as far as possible, the usual pattern of life and work on the Estate was maintained. The head gardener still sent prize-winning fruit and blooms to flower and agricultural shows such as the Chelsea Flower Show. In September 1915 Sunny received a silver medal for his dahlias from the National Dahlia Society.

Of course many servants went to war but those too old for action continued with the usual tasks. The chimneys were swept by Mr Morgan and the many hundreds of windows were cleaned by the Farley family. Mr Buckingham continued to look after the Palace clocks and the Reverend Clark played the Willis organ in the Long Library. Funds and subscriptions were regularly sent to a variety of institutions such as the Woodstock Fat Stock Show and the Almswomen's Garden Fund. Repairs

Local hero George Woodford and Christina McDuff on their wedding day.

on Estate buildings continued to be never-ending, cottages and farm buildings were painted and thatched and the Park walls were repaired. Trees were felled and the wood carted. At Christmas each year the Estate workers received their joints of beef and after Christmas the cesspits in the garden were emptied.

Sunny spent a lot of time away from Blenheim during the war but when at home he liked the Palace to be run as he expected it should be and whilst butlers in other great houses may have had to make do with women serving at table, such a travesty never occurred at Blenheim.

The Armistice was declared at 11 o'clock in the morning, on 11 November 1918. For the men at the front the silence of this sudden peace was quite shocking. At home, the Armistice triggered countrywide celebrations and heartfelt relief that the war was over.

At the time of the Armistice the family were scattered far and wide. The Duchess, Consuelo, was in Paris where she attended a party to mark the end of the war. Sunny was also in France with his son Lord Ivor; his older son, Lord Blandford was in hospital in St Andrews in Scotland. Winston Churchill had spent the months leading up to the Armistice travelling between France and England. On Armistice Day he was in London and in the evening dined with Lloyd George, F.E. Smith and Sir Henry Wilson. Around the table there was a discussion about what should be done with the Kaiser. Lloyd George wanted him shot.

At Blenheim the main celebrations to mark the end of the war took place at Christmas. A large party of friends and family gathered to mark Christmas, the end of the war and the 'coming of age' of the Duke's oldest son, Lord Blandford. He had by then recovered enough to keep up with the rest of the family, which was useful as the frivolities included a paper chase on horseback.

During the Duke's lifetime great estates across the land experienced change, sometimes unwelcome change and this was particularly so during and after the First World War. Many had to be sold, the revenues from the farms no longer able to support the great house, or because all the male heirs had been killed at the Front. Blenheim survived, largely thanks to the substantial injection of cash brought across from America by Consuelo, but it also survived because of Sunny's care and close attention to detail. He was a man of his time, a great Victorian. He inherited a Victorian Estate on the brink of collapse. When he died the Blenheim Estate was set fair for the modern era.

5

Embellishments

The Great Court and the Terraces

With the financial settlement made by Consuelo's father in the form of a very generous dowry, the Duke had the funds necessary to fulfil his long-held wish to restore and beautify Blenheim. He wasted no time in getting started and a considerable amount of money was spent decorating the interior of Blenheim and in creating, outside, a setting worthy of the place.

He transformed the view from the Palace windows looking out to the north, east and west. This transformation was to prove his life's work. Had he lived he may well have turned his attention to the South Lawn. It was Sacheverell Sitwell, the writer, who suggested to him that, after the Water Terraces, his next project should be to re-establish the Great Parterre. Henry Wise had planted, for the 1st Duke, an enormous parterre to the south of the Palace. During the time of the 4th Duke Lancelot 'Capability' Brown had swept away what little was left of this Parterre and planted an extensive lawn in its place. In reply to Sacheverell Sitwell's suggestion Sunny had simply smiled and shrugged. By then he was ill and possibly knew that he did not have the time for such a large project.

The present head gardener at Blenheim, Mrs Hilary Wood, was once asked if she would like to see the Great Parterre re-established. She immediately said that it would take an enormous number of 'gardener hours' to maintain such a garden and where would the cricket pitch go? Both she and the Blenheim cricket team are thankful that the South Lawn was left as Brown had designed.

Great Court laid to lawn in a design drawn up by Lancelot 'Capability' Brown. Shortly after this picture was taken the lawns were dug up ready for the workmen to restore the courtyard to Vanbrugh's original plan of stones and cobbles.

The first of Sunny's major external embellishments was the restoration of Great Court to its original design of gravel and cobbles, as built for the 1st Duke. To do this the oval lawn and side lawns laid by 'Capability' Brown were dug up and the side stone terraces, which had also been removed by Brown, had to be rebuilt. Sunny had pre-Brown prints showing how Great Court had looked in its original design, so it was a relatively straightforward project in terms of deciding what the new layout should look like. Achille Duchêne, the French landscape architect, oversaw the work, which was actually done by a local builder, Mr Tolley and his workmen. Mr Tolley regularly worked for the Duke on all kinds of building-related problems and projects, so it was natural that he was brought in to deal with Great Court. The Duke gave Mr Tolley an 18th Century engraving of the north front of the Palace, which showed Great Court as it had been originally constructed and this was used as a guide and a plan.

The Palace estate ledgers show that stone from the Taynton Quarry in the Cotswolds along with Portland Stone was used to rebuild Great

Digging up Great Court with the side terracing taking shape.

Court. This was perfectly in keeping, as when the Palace was first built, Taynton Quarry had supplied a large proportion of the stone. Portland Stone had been used to build the steps going up to the north and south fronts. When the courtyard was complete the last job was to lay the gravel. Mr Smart was paid £1.12.6 for carting the gravel and Mr Walker was paid £0.7.6 for rolling it flat.

In addition to re-establishing the main structure of Great Court, many of the stone decorative sculptures that had once graced Great Court, were, by the early 1900s, missing. Mr Kibble, a stonemason from the nearby village of Charlbury, carved the urn-finials which to this day stand on the colonnades. A couple of the originals still existed so Mr Kibble was able to produce copies. From France Sunny ordered six statues to line the roof on either side of the North Portico. When these statues were ready, in June 1907, Messrs. Symons & Co were paid £21.7.6 for 'carriage of statues'. Sunny did not construct the gates into Great Court according to Vanbrugh's original plans, so the work in Great Court did not represent a complete restoration. He did install the beautiful North Gates which are still in use today, by the family and their private guests. Messrs. Farley and Son, who had been hard at work painting and decorating inside the Palace, painted the railings across the Courtyard. Sunny also had a large ditch dug either side of these gates in order to stop deer from entering Great Court. He was particularly irritated by deer and eventually had them banned from the Park.

Sunny was very pleased with the finished work and had a stone placed in Great Court bearing the inscription:

> This court was restored by Charles Richard John Spencer-Churchill, Duke of Marlborough, under the guidance of M. Duchêne, Architect, 1900–1910.

Before Great Court was completely finished, Sunny and Duchêne turned their attention to the east front and to what today is the present Duke's

The east front garden before Sunny started work on his new Italian Garden.

Sunny's Italian Garden.

The Waldo Story fountain in the Italian Garden.

private garden, the Italian Garden. Sunny wanted a formal garden. There was already a formal garden in place so it is surprising that he felt the need for a complete re-design. Duchêne kept the same rectangular shape and size but designed a new garden which would have around the sides, swirling scroll-like patterns in dwarf box hedging. Around the outside of these he placed stand-alone examples of topiary. Today the gardeners still have fun with the topiary but there is now a hedge in between the topiary birds and moles. The plan for the garden also included statues and orange trees planted in large tubs. This was a reference to the fact that this garden had, on one side, the Orangery. In the centre of the garden the plan called for a round pool. The Duke commissioned the sculptor, Waldo Story, to design a statue for the centre of this pool. He created a beautiful fountain of a gilded Venus holding a Ducal Coronet. This has recently been restored and regilded and looks magnificent. The paths in the garden were made of crushed red brick to contrast with the green of the box hedging. When finished Duchêne had built an elegant, formal but very beautiful garden and it remains so today.

The transformation of the garden on the west side of the Palace, into new Water Terraces, began in 1925. Sunny and Gladys followed the construction with great interest and in Sunny's case with determined direction. He had the whole process photographed and his wife also took her camera to record the remarkable changes that were finally completed in 1932. These photographs are kept in three huge albums on a shelf in the Gallery above the Long Library. They give a step-by-step pictorial record of how the building project was completed and the problems that were

The completed Water Terraces

encountered along the way. At the end of the third and last album there is a beautiful picture of the completed terraces. The water is still and the new hedging looks like tracery in a window. Sunny wrote a somewhat melancholy endnote in the album:

> For various reasons I have not had the heart or courage to write an account of the six years labour and study that I have devoted in superintending the work on these terraces. Perhaps I will write one day – but let not the reader assume that this work was simple, that any architect could have done it. The result is the combination of brains, knowledge of technique, and culture of two men working in harmony. These two men have left the Park – East and West fronts of Blenheim – in perfect architectural design – a worthy frame to the Palace. M.M.1933

The two men referred to by Sunny were himself and Achille Duchêne, who worked on the north front and the Italian Gardens before the First World War. It was a deliberate choice to employ a French landscape architect as Sunny admired the gardens of Versailles and felt the Palace needed just such a formal setting to enhance the remarkable English Baroque architecture. Indeed, the two men visited Versailles together as part of

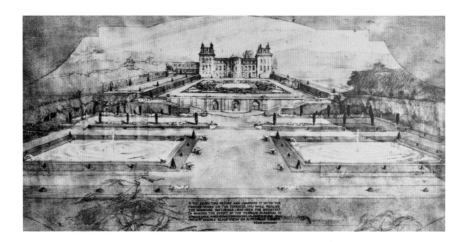

Duchene's original drawing for the Water Terraces. The plans are in Blenheim archives.

The west front before the start of the Water Terraces.

the preparation for this major project, walking round discussing what they felt were shortcomings and advantages to Le Nôtre's famous garden. Sunny did not want a copy of these French gardens but he admired the formal nature of such design. He also gave Duchêne the instruction

The workmen ready to make a start on the Water Terraces 1925.

By February 1926 great progress had been made on the Water Terraces.

that he was to 'inspire' his design with 'a feeling of joyousness, for joy means the birth of everything; of spirit, of hope and aspiration.' It was perhaps not too surprising that he was in need of a garden that would raise his spirits. Life with Gladys was proving very difficult.

Beginning to construct a retaining wall on the Chapel side of the uppermost water terrace.

The building of the Water Terraces required the construction of strong, deep and thick retaining walls on all sides.

On the west of the Palace Duchêne found a large lawned area bordered by shrubbery with some mature trees. The area was largely flat with a gentle slope which then led to a more dramatic slope down to the lakeside. After much discussion the plan eventually settled upon was for two large terraces linked by a decorated retaining wall, two grand flights of steps and a third narrow, shallow terrace.

By February 1926 the workmen were assembled on the west front for a photograph and the scene in the background shows work well under way. A track had been laid to facilitate the movement of earth and stone. Next to a photograph labelled 'Dec 1926' there is a handwritten note stating: 'We dug out about 20,000 cubic yards of soil on Terrace No. 1.2.3.' Small wonder that they needed a railway line! At the outset large retaining walls were built on each side where originally there had been sloping shrubberies. To build these walls deep trenches were dug for the concrete bases and an enormous amount of earth was moved.

It soon became apparent that the area where the men were working was not an easy site and the build was not without its problems. In August 1926 the bank which led down to the lake slipped. Sunny noted that the men had to work very quickly to 'get the bank at a safe angle'. To make matters worse the ground was poor and there was only a very thin layer of soil and beneath this was stone which made excavation problematic. He joked that: 'the terrace is really a stone quarry.'

As the project progressed, adaptations were made to the original plans. In 1926 during a major period of construction he noted that: 'The Chapel Terrace (the Upper Terrace) was reduced in height so that the view of the Lake from the Palace was not spoilt.' Construction continued throughout 1927 and by August photographs show the development of the steps from the Chapel Terrace to the lower terraces.

In the autumn of 1928 the project progressed from major construction towards embellishment. Sunny and Duchêne discussed specific points of decoration. Rather surprisingly, given that he had employed a French architect, he wrote to Duchêne saying: 'We must be careful not to decorate in the French style.' At that time he was taking exception to Duchêne's preference for tall, narrow trees. Preferring the use of sculpture he purchased six marble columns upon which were placed the six statues of winged victories. Of this he said to Duchêne 'These columns really replace the perpendicular trees which you put in your original design.' They also disagreed on the large pots Sunny placed on the lowest terrace, the Lake Terrace. Clearly Sunny prevailed as the pots are still there today. There was also disagreement over the issue of still or moving water. While Duchêne favoured fountains, the Duke did not

December 1926

The stone that was taken out of the ground during the construction of the Water Terraces was used for the roads in the Park.

saying: 'Limpidity of water is pleasing and possesses a romance.'[1] He went on to make the forcible point that any public park could give 'a vulgar display of waterworks'.

Despite these discussions and disagreements the Duke was generous in his praise of Duchêne concerning the overall impact and design of the terraces. In 1929 Sunny wrote to him saying:

> The ensemble of the Terraces is magnificent and in my judgement far superior to the work done by Le Notre [sic] at Versailles. The proportion of the house, the Terrace and the Lake is perfect.

High praise indeed!

There was still much work to be done in 1929 and that was when the sculptor made a start on the caryatids, which were completed in December of the same year.[2] The pools on the Chapel Terrace and the lowest terrace, the Lake Terrace, had been dug and shaped by late 1928 but

Sunny keeping a close eye on the Water Terraces as construction entered the decorative stage. This photo shows that urns, statues and lawns were put in place whilst a certain amount of construction continued.

they had not been filled with water. In November 1928 the controversial stone pots were placed on the lower terraces and in December 1929 the large statues were winched into place in the four corners on the Chapel Terrace. They were not placed on plinths at this point. As photographs taken at the time show, the pools in the Chapel Terrace and third lowest terrace were by then filled with water and slightly different in shape from the final construction; the lowest terrace pools were octagonal in shape and not embellished with statues as they are now.

In January 1930 a new phase of construction began in earnest and the pools in the lowest terrace were drained, reshaped into rectangles and lined with concrete. The Bernini fountain was then reassembled in the middle of one of the pools. This was a major project as the Bernini fountain required considerable restoration before it could be placed in the pool. Next to a photo of the Bernini fountain is a note:

> The fountain... was terribly damaged. The figures in marble were partially broken. They had to be sent to London to Farmer and Brindley,

(above) The photographs in the three albums suggest that between 1928 and 1929 there was a slight pause for thought. This picture shows the lower terrace shaped and filled with water before it was drained and dug to a rectangle shape and lined with concrete.

(left) The Bernini fountain in the gardens before it was moved to the lower water terrace.

where it took nearly two years to get the marble free from decay due to damp and neglect.

By October 1930 both pools were once more filled with water but the pool on the left had no central feature to match the Bernini fountain. This was added later to provide a balance to the Bernini fountain. It was

January 1930 digging out the lower terrace and creating depth for the two fountains; one was the Bernini fountain, moved from below the Cascade, and the second was meant to be made to match, but was in fact much simpler in design.

also at this time that the two sphinxes were added to the second terrace. Both of these sphinxes carry the face of Gladys Deacon. It is not known what she herself thought of this as relations between Sunny and his wife were rather strained at that time.

In January 1931 work moved to the Chapel Terrace and these pools were drained and excavated to what appears to be a much deeper level than before. The pools were lined with concrete. In December 1931 the statues were raised on to plinths in the four corners of the Chapel Terrace. The area around the pools was then planted into intricate patterns and the pools were filled with water from Rosamund's Well. Gladys followed this phase of the construction very closely with her camera and her spaniels. One of her photographs shows a spaniel surveying the site and it is labelled 'Little Snowflake April 1931'. By 1932 the photographs show that the terraces were complete. They were as Sunny had wished, an elegant and sophisticated setting for the Palace. He thought they were beautiful and had an inscription made in stone and placed on the Chapel wall which read, 'Achille Duchêne, Architect, to whose genius posterity enjoys the beauty of these terraces'. It is to be hoped that he gained

The lower water terrace showing the Bernini Fountain in place with the second pool as yet empty of a matching fountain.

much pleasure from them because little else at that time gave him joy. His health was declining and his marriage to Gladys was, by then, far beyond repair.

The final word on the Water Terraces must perhaps go to Father Martindale speaking at the Duke's funeral service in 1934. He said:

> The very terraces that he built at Blenheim… were due not in the least to a desire for self-commemoration, but to his appreciation that the house needed that pedestal, as indeed it did.

The Park

Blenheim Park is soaked in history. Centuries before the advent of Vanbrugh's stonemasons and 'Capability' Brown created his exquisite lakeside landscapes, to the north of the marshy, meandering Glyme valley, Roman legions once crunched their way down Akeman Street on their long march from St Albans to Cirencester. One thousand years later Plantagenet Kings hunted their deerhounds from Woodstock Palace. It was King Henry I who initially enclosed Woodstock Park as a hunting forest and built the original manor house. His son, King Henry II, expanded the manor into a full-scale royal palace which in turn was

The scene before the water was added to the upper terrace.

Digging out the upper terrace (or Chapel Terrace) and lining the pools with concrete. This work started in earnest in January 1931.

The medieval forest is centred around High Lodge, once the home of the Ranger of the ancient royal hunting park.

much enhanced by King Henry III with extensive chapels and outbuildings. After the Civil War Woodstock Palace was allowed to decay until, finally, its ruins were swept under the Grand Bridge as foundation rubble by the 1st Duchess of Marlborough. Her husband, John Churchill, had been granted the Royal Woodstock hunting park by a grateful nation for his military victories in the Wars of the Spanish Succession.

When Sunny commenced his ambitious planting programme at the turn of the twentieth century, the presence of the medieval forest with its ancient oaks and surrounding carpet of bracken was never far from his thoughts. He was determined at all times to preserve the atmosphere and unique characteristics of the existing Park. The Park can broadly be divided into two distinct parts, the romantic medieval forest focussed on High Lodge to the south-west and the grand formality of the age of Queen Anne represented by elm avenues running north from the Palace towards Ditchley Gate. Sunny wrote in his 'Tree Planting Book', where he recorded his remarkable conservation achievements:

> The old park where the oaks and bracken exist was meant to remain as an example to all time of the imposing effect of the medieval forest. In a similar way the Monument and Lower Park where elms were planted in avenues was meant to convey to the observer the idea and style of the age of Queen Anne and the eighteenth century, the period when Blenheim was built.

An ancient oak by the Lake at Blenheim. Sunny commissioned Henry Taunt to photograph the gardens and Park in 1896. This photograph is from an album of Taunt's photographs kept, today, in a bookcase on the private side of the Palace.

Sunny was particularly critical of some of his ducal ancestors whose haphazard planting on the Estate had had such a dire effect on the parkland landscape. He wrote in his 'Tree Book':

> I then examined with regret the results of the planting carried out by those who were responsible for the arrangement of the trees during the nineteenth century. They have been arranged in an aimless fashion and it appears as if this important subject has been left to the caprice of incompetent foresters and to the will of unintelligent estate agents. In order to avoid the errors of the past I caused this book to be drawn up and insist that therein careful entries are made.

Sunny thereby demonstrates the same eye for detail and impeccable taste as he did within the Palace and the Gardens.

Nowhere were these qualities better demonstrated than with his ornamental lakeside plantings. In 1896 following the dredging of the lake he

Trees were taken from the Blenheim nurseries and were replanted across the estate and gardens.

planted clumps of copper beech and cedars alongside Bladon Water. He wrote in the 'Tree Book':

> The ground was covered by eight inches of silt which was drawn by steam power out of the river in the summer of 1896. Prior to planting the ground was double dug to a depth of eighteen inches thus the silt and the soil became well intermixed. The clumps were permanently fenced in with good three nailed iron standard fencing and with wire netting inside.

And now his aesthetic nature manifests itself:

> I planted these clumps hoping to get the following effect, that a person passing Bladon Bridge will first see a mass of copper beech, followed by another mass of grey, glaucous cedars and again beyond, another mass of copper beech. I like to think that a combination of the two colours, the copper and the grey, ought to be most effective and picturesque.

*The Monument Avenue looking south. Little could Sunny know that in
two generations his endeavours would be destroyed by a beetle.*

A year later, in a similar vein, he planted clumps astride the main lake
north of the Grand Bridge. He wrote:

> The large copper beeches were grown on the border of Norton Heath
> and were conveyed a distance of four miles to the site of the old Manor
> House. The ground was covered with mud removed from the Queen Pool
> to a depth of one foot six inches to two foot below which there was only
> nine inches of soil under which was building rubbish and rubble.

The connoisseur Duke continued: 'These copper beeches will be most
effective in years to come if seen from the entrance gate to the Park.' At
the same time he introduced poplars, dogwood and golden elder onto
the island knowing that they would grow well as they were planted on
mud taken from the lake: 'I cut down most of the rubbish growing on the
island and the trees planted should do uncommonly well.'

In 1898 he turned his attention to the unique ancient woodland in

High Park planting 148 large well-grown oaks 'well-guarded against deer and rabbits'. His entry in the 'Tree Book' reads:

> I hope to preserve the effect of this Forest of the Middle Ages. It appears to me that no oak trees have been planted in it for 150 years which is a great pity. Many of the old oaks are dying. The planting of oaks in the High Park should continue for another 25 years and then the Park should be stocked for 500 years to come.

But perhaps his tour de force came in 1901 when not only did he establish clumps of beech and horse chestnut across the Park to augment 'Capability' Brown's plantings but he also replanted the celebrated Monument Avenue that was irresponsibly cut down some time in the nineteenth century. There were eight avenues in total comprising four double rows. He notes:

> The idea of a double avenue is to protect trees from the wind. The double avenue is meant to grow together giving at a distance the effect of one line of trees instead of two. Any man who cuts these trees down for the purpose of selling the timber is a Scoundrel and deserves the worst state that can befall him. In the year 2000 it will be a remarkable feature of the Park extending as it does for nearly two miles.

The Low Park Avenue in the snow.

The view of the Lake from Rosamund's Well in 1896.

Little could Sunny know that within a few generations his endeavours would be destroyed by a beetle which in turn would force his grandson to replant the Avenue with lime trees.

If Sunny had an artistic temperament he was also a pragmatist. As early as 1893 he planted 300 horse chestnuts in the Pleasure Grounds above the cascade: 'To make the garden more private from the view of people walking in the Park.' They all came from the Blenheim Nursery opposite Spring Lock Cottage and were eight to ten feet tall. He loved his field sports and consequently planted thousands of trees across the Estate to enhance its shooting potential. The main quarry was the grey partridge, now sadly near extinction in Oxfordshire as a result of modern farming practices. In 1906 he planted trees alongside existing hedges at Hordley Farm, the object being: 'to thicken the fences for partridge nesting and to increase the hedge height to drive the birds over'.

In 1895 he planted a narrow belt between Ditchley Gate and North Farm noting:

> These trees (Larch, Spruce and Scots Fir) were planted for the purposes of enabling me to drive partridges, they are not considered ornamental.

They were planted in land which was in a good state of cultivation and the whole field was wired to protect it from ground game. On account of this no wire netting was erected when planting and the cost was much reduced.

At Akeman Street and Coombe Manor Farms high hedges were planted over which to drive the partridges and 'the whole of the ground planted was enclosed so that any nests shall be safe from lurching dogs and foxes.' At much the same time he planted yew, box, laurel and blackthorn on the Lince Bank to thicken the bottom of existing beech clumps for his pheasants. As with his decoration of the State Rooms in the Palace, Sunny was not afraid to admit his mistakes. In 1894 he established three larch and spruce plantations for game cover near Fourteen Acre Clump in the Monument Park. He wrote in his 'Tree Book':

I made a mistake in planting these clumps. They are un-picturesque and I doubt whether they will do well in this spot.

But thankfully the majority of Sunny's plantings did thrive. It was an immense undertaking, well planned and skilfully executed, proving him a worthy successor to the genius of 'Capability' Brown. By the time he felt his project was complete, just after the First World War had ended, Sunny had planted some 465,000 trees at a total cost of £7,736 (£850,000 in today's values).

The Lake
As soon as the marriage settlement with the Vanderbilt family was agreed in 1895, gifting Sunny $2,500,000 (£64,000,000 in today's values) of railway stock and an annual income of $100,000, he sent a telegram to the Blenheim Estate Office instructing his agent to 'Dredge the Lake'. The boggy Glyme valley which had played host to both Woodstock and Blenheim Palaces over the centuries was about to undergo its third makeover.

The initial designs for Blenheim Lake were drawn up by Colonel Armstrong, the 1st Duke's chief military engineer and completed in 1724. These included a lake to the Woodstock side of the Grand Bridge, dammed by a stone wall running across to the old Manor House by way of the existing island and a series of waterfalls and canals which ran

(top left) The Lower Bladon lake showing serious signs of silting before it was dredged in 1896. (bottom left) The new bridge built by William Chambers for the 4th Duke of Marlborough. Silt spreading in the foreground following dredging. It was here that Sunny planted his copper beech and cedar clumps that look so splendid today. (top right) Steam engines working on dredging Bladon Lake. (bottom right) Lower Bladon Lake after dredging.

under the bridge down to the site of the existing cascade. In 1763 the 4th Duke commissioned 'Capability' Brown for a major landscaping project at Blenheim which would last a decade and include perhaps his greatest masterpiece, the current lake and cascade. The latter was completed by 1770 by which time Brown had turned his attention to the lower lake near Bladon. By 1773 he had widened the River Glyme into its sweeping serpentine form and constructed an additional cascade at the point where the Glyme joins the larger River Evenlode below the Lince. The total cost for the whole project at Blenheim, including planting, was £21,000. One hundred and twenty years later both Blenheim Lake to the east of the Grand Bridge and Bladon Lake to the south of New Bridge had silted up to unsatisfactory levels. Sunny was compelled to take action, not just for aesthetic reasons but also to alleviate the dangers of flooding.

A contract was signed on 21 January 1896 with John Fell of Leamington to remove 200,000 cubic yards of silt from the Queen Pool down to a depth of four feet at an estimated cost of £10,000 to £12,000. The silt was excavated by bucket operated between two steam engines and then conveyed by a tramway system from Fisheries Cottage to the Rifle Range valley above Icehouse Clump. Most of the Queen Pool at this stage was covered by weeds owing to the shallow water, however, the area of sedge reeds running up to Seven Arches Bridge where the Glyme enters the lake was to remain in situ. The contract had to be completed by 30 April at which date only 130,000 cubic yards had been excavated. There were also unacceptable cost overruns which together with the delays forced Sunny to terminate the contract. A new engineer (Brown) and contractor (The South Western Steam Cultivation Company) were brought in and Fell settled out of court. A new contract was signed on 17 July and the work was completed within nine weeks. The total cost of the two contracts for cleaning out the Queen Pool was £16,702,7s,6d (£2,100,000 in todays values). In addition it was deemed necessary to make minor repairs to the Grand Bridge stonework. £150 covered the costs of the stonemasons.

The Bladon Lake was also excavated in the summer of 1896. The cost of dredging 1,170 yards downstream of New Bridge with a width of 50 yards and to a depth of 2.5 feet came to £1,664. The cost of two engines and a scoop was fifteen shillings an hour and Sunny's eye for detail was again in evidence as the contract stated that a timekeeper was required to deduct every minute lost when the engines ceased operating by way of breakdown or meal times. The silt was spread on the banks and allowed to dry. On the north bank some four acres were steam cultivated and ploughed with horses into an arable field. On the south bank Sunny planted his now much admired ornamental clumps of copper beeches and cedars.

The interior of the Palace

No sooner had the Blenheim Estate Office received an instruction to dredge the Lake in the summer of 1895 than another directive was issued requesting the commencement of extensive redecorations within the Palace. Time was tight as the Prince and Princess of Wales were coming to stay for a shooting weekend the following autumn and there had been few improvements at the Palace in terms of comfort and decoration over the latter half of the nineteenth century. Indeed, when Sunny inherited, Blenheim only had one bathroom.

The young Duke decided to sweep away some of the Victorian gloom and called in the services of two local decorators. Farley and Son were contracted to undertake the more basic work of painting and papering the family bedrooms, servant's quarters, kitchen, pantry, scullery, basement, dairymaid's rooms and electrician lodges while the more sophisticated work of painting the windows and Chapel ceiling was carried out by J.H. Kingerlee.

The Prince had specifically asked the Marlboroughs if he could visit Blenheim. Although Queen Victoria was a close friend of Sunny's

The south end of the Long Library showing the statue of Queen Anne and the fact that there were no books and no book cases.

A photograph taken of the Duke entertaining friends in the Long Library c.1925, showing the book cases in the background, which housed Sunny's new library.

grandfather, the proposed royal visit was the first such occasion since George III had been entertained by the 4th Duke. As such Sunny was not going to hold back on household expenditure. He refurbished the three State Rooms in between the Saloon and Long Library with French chairs and Boulle cabinets.3 He then redecorated the rooms 'with gilded boiseries in the manner of Versailles.' The latter involved twenty craftsmen from Paris working at Blenheim for over six months. Later in life he regretted his decision telling his architect, Achille Duchêne:

> When I was young and uninformed I put French decoration into the three state rooms here. The rooms have English proportions with the result being that the French decoration is quite out of scale which leaves an unpleasant impression on those who possess trained eyes.

But as ever Sunny was a perfectionist and art historian Robin Fedden wrote in the *Country House Guide*, 'the pastiche is accomplished and the craftsmanship meticulous.'

After the State Rooms were completed Sunny turned his attention to the Long Library which stretches along the entirety of the west side of the Palace. Until 1882 it had housed the Sunderland Library, one of the most famous libraries in the world and assembled by Charles Spencer, 3rd Earl of Sunderland who married the 1st Duke's daughter, Lady Anne Churchill. The 7th Duke had always been short of funds to maintain the Palace and to support his ducal lifestyle and as a result was forced to sell the family heirlooms. In December 1881 the first of two auction sales took place, each lasting ten days, which raised in total some £56,000. The 7th Duke then received a grant of £2,000 to turn the Library into a picture gallery which for a short period displayed Van Dyck's Equestrian Charles I. Following the sale of the exceptional Blenheim picture collection by his father in 1885, Sunny decided to replace the bookcases, purchasing in the process, numerous expensively bound books. The Library then became a focal point for dances and family entertainment.

Although Sunny was a connoisseur of works of art, paintings were not his speciality. He left this pursuit to his two wives who both became educated collectors in their own right having a passionate interest in the French Impressionist painters. He did acquire several pieces of Boulle furniture. Although he did not acquire paintings he did commission several important portraits. The magnificent family portrait by John Singer Sargent, painted in 1905 and displayed opposite the 4th Duke's family by Reynolds, is undoubtedly his greatest bequest to the interior of the Palace. He also commissioned Umberto Veruda to paint portraits of himself, Bert and Ivor in 1903, Alfred Munnings to paint Ivor and himself with the 'Blenheim Greys' in the Quorn country (exhibited at the Royal Academy in 1924) and Giovanni Boldini to paint Gladys in 1916.

In both the Veruda and Munnings portraits Sunny was painted in full hunting attire which depict another personal characteristic. He was a dapper man, an immaculate dresser and was always well turned out whether on the hunting field or at home out on the Estate. Munnings wrote in his autobiography:

> There were moments during the Duke's sitting when I called upon my inner man to make the extra effort, so exquisite and traditionally correct were his scarlet cut-away coat, his white leathers, flesh coloured tops and long stirrup-leathers.

6

Public life

Maiden speech 1895

Sunny Marlborough delivered his maiden speech in the House of Lords from the Conservative benches on 15 August 1895 by moving the Loyal Address in reply to the Queen's Speech. One must assume that such an honour being bestowed on one so young should be attributed as much to his perceived future promise as to his famous dynastic background. Hansard reported: 'he wore the uniform of the Oxfordshire Yeomanry and was received with cheers.' He began his speech by reminding their Lordships how successfully 'both wings of the great Unionist party' had worked together in Opposition and that this harmonious working relationship boded well for their forthcoming joint period in government.

He moved on to cover various aspects of foreign policy, notably a review of Britain's commitments in the Far East, in addition to advocating a progressive policy for Ireland. He reminded the House that Britain's relations with the other great powers were currently satisfactory enough not to threaten the peace of Europe but with great perception he pointed out that there was a lesson to be learned from the conclusion of the Sino-Japanese war, namely that naval power would be of prime importance to Britain's future national security. With Tirpitz shortly to be appointed head of the German Navy and supplied with a brief from the Kaiser to build a battle fleet to match the British, this surely demonstrated commendable foresight. Sunny concluded with a very personal appeal for the government to rally behind an ailing agricultural sector,

Sunny immaculately turned out in the uniform of the Queen's Own Oxfordshire Hussars at camp in Blenheim Park c1900.

'speaking with conviction as a landowner and one who is deeply interested in the affairs of agriculture.' Not unnaturally, with time, farming would become his special subject.

The Leader of the Liberal Opposition, Lord Rosebery, with cherished memories of his close friend, Lord Randolph Churchill welling-up in his subconscious, rose to congratulate Sunny:

> The Mover spoke with a singular vivacity and with a grace which I am sure charmed your Lordships and gave you reason to hope that he will not unworthily bear his illustrious name or fall in any way short of the traditions of that brilliant uncle of his whose loss his Party and even more his friends outside his Party had so deeply to deplore in the earlier part of this year.

Working his way up the political ladder with the grassroots. Sunny hosting the Association of Conservative Party Chairmen at Blenheim c1898.

The Prime Minister, Lord Salisbury, then rose and also congratulated the Mover and Seconder (Lord Ampthill):

> May I be permitted to rejoice that two of the hereditary members of this House bearing names amongst the most illustrious of those which it contains have shown so much power of debate and so high a promise of future eloquence and fame.

Paymaster General's Office
In the autumn of 1899, after a relatively short political apprenticeship, Sunny was launched on his ministerial career by Lord Salisbury, the Prime Minister, when granted the Office of Paymaster General. As evidenced

by Consuelo writing in *The Glitter and the Gold*, it was not the most illustrious junior ministerial promotion yet it was a start:

> In 1899 Marlborough was named Paymaster General of the Forces, a post his famous ancestor had found lucrative but which no longer held the same perquisites unless attending service in Christopher Wren's lovely chapel of the Royal Hospital in Chelsea could be considered such.

It is worth examining why the Prime Minister offered Sunny a government position at the tender age of twenty-eight. The young Duke had certainly created a favourable impression amongst his fellow peers, coming across as a committed and assiduous member of the House. It is also possible that in the back of his mind, Lord Salisbury felt a tinge of guilt for accepting the resignation of Sunny's brilliant yet wayward uncle, Lord Randolph Churchill, as Chancellor of the Exchequer in December 1886. This rash decision proved political suicide for Lord Randolph. It ruined a meteoric political career and he died in February 1895 only a few months before Sunny's maiden speech. Maybe a kindly Salisbury saw some of Randolph's better qualities in his young nephew and in granting Sunny promotion found a subtle way of repaying a debt of gratitude to the Churchill family for Randolph's services to the Conservative Party? Lord Salisbury had been a close friend of Sunny's grandmother, Fanny Marlborough, so the whole affair must have been an embarrassment for the Prime Minister.

The Paymaster General's Office came into being as a new government department with its own political head in 1836 but there was nothing new about its functions. The office represented a consolidation, bringing together four pay offices which had been in existence for 150 years within various branches of the armed services, namely, Paymaster General of the Forces, Paymaster and Treasurer of the Chelsea Hospital, Treasurer of the Ordnance and Treasurer of the Navy.

As the Victorian era drew to a close staff dropped to below seventy, less than two-thirds of which were clerks. About 20,000 pensions were on the books and around 400,000 payments were made a year. In 1899 the Office of Paymaster General was given the task of paying an entirely new class of pensioner, the former teachers of elementary schools. In his pamphlet on 'The Story of the Paymaster General's Office 1836-1986', Colin Ulph wrote:

In 1899 the then Prime Minister, Lord Salisbury, launched Sunny's ministerial career by granting him the office of Paymaster General.

In 1852 the post began to be held jointly with other departmental appointments and at once the PGO was relegated to the back seat with day to day control passing formally to a civil servant, the Assistant Paymaster General, under power of attorney while the Minister attended to more pressing duties.

Lord Monteagle commented caustically in mid-Victorian times:

> The Office of Paymaster General is at present only nominal – a mere sinecure – no salary is paid but his remuneration is fully equal to the services rendered.

This, no doubt, explains how Sunny found the time to depart for the South African War for six months in 1900 while continuing to hold down his ministerial position. The experience of active service must have assisted the young duke in making a competent debut at the dispatch box on 25 March 1901 when he replied to Lord Monkswell on the question of pensions for disabled soldiers. The Paymaster General was also Chairman of the Board of the Chelsea Hospital Commissioners who in turn were charged with granting pensions to soldiers discharged from the service. Monkswell, an ex-commissioner, was concerned that pensions paid to soldiers who had been discharged from the army for either wounds received in action or through sickness as a result of service in the field might be inadequate.

Sunny explained to the House that following the Boer War wounded soldiers would receive with immediate effect the maximum grant available (two shillings and six pence a day) and that henceforth no sliding scales dependent on class of injury would apply. In his opinion, by erring on the generous side, injured servicemen would recover more quickly and therefore be able to return to civil employment at an earlier date. In a similar fashion soldiers discharged for sickness in the field also had their daily entitlements increased thereby hopefully enabling an accelerated recovery and benefiting the Treasury over the long term. He concluded by telling the Lords that he had tried to award these pensions 'in a liberal and generous spirit' in the hope that such action would encourage and assist future recruitment within the armed forces.

Lord High Steward

We are reminded time and again by Consuelo that Sunny took his ducal responsibilities very seriously. To this young, liberal minded American, he must have appeared an almost feudal figure dwelling at the apex of a hierarchical society in which the differences in rank were most important. In 1902 he became just that, maybe the grandest and most favoured aristocrat in the realm. That summer he was not only made a Knight of the Garter but also Lord High Steward at the Coronation of King Edward VII.

Lord High Steward is the first of the Grand Offices of State. One can quite understand why Winston Churchill, his cousin, commenced Sunny's obituary with the words: 'During his childhood and his father's life he was unhappy but when in 1892 he became Duke, life opened very brilliantly for him.' The Office has remained vacant since 1421 except at coronations when the Lord High Steward bears the St Edward's Crown

Sunny was Lord High Steward at the Coronation of King Edward VII in 1902,
and at the time the most favoured aristocrat in the realm, Winston wrote:-
'When he became Duke life opened very brilliantly for him.

in the royal procession to the altar and during trials of peers in the House of Lords when the Lord High Steward presides. In the latter situation the Lord Chancellor was usually appointed to act as Lord High Steward.

Even though Sunny's duties were less than arduous, it is little wonder that he stood down as Paymaster General on 11 March. The coronation was scheduled for June but then postponed to August because of the future King's serious illness from appendicitis. Why was Sunny given the Garter at the age of thirty? Lord Salisbury certainly did not think the young duke deserved such an honour. Consuelo writes of a visit to Hatfield that summer:

> With a twinkle in his eye Lord Salisbury approached the reason for our visit. 'I am, I believe', he said, 'to present the Order of the Garter to the Duke but I have not the slightest reason wherefore'. Sorely tempted to reply with the old quip, 'We know there is no damned merit to it', I nevertheless abstained.

And why indeed, was the Duke given the highest office of state, Lord High Steward, for the Coronation?

Royal patronage

We must assume that Sunny was held in high esteem by the future King Edward VII. On initial reflection this might seem rather strange following the court dramas of the Aylesford Affair a generation earlier, brought on by the disreputable behaviour of Sunny's father and Uncle Randolph. Edward VII was obviously a kindly and forgiving personality and may have seen much of himself in Sunny's character. The patriotic Duke adhered strictly to protocol, had a weakness for pageantry and was thrilled by the pomp and ceremony of ancient tradition. Besides, he was the only 'commoner' to live in his own palace, where he had lavishly entertained the Prince of Wales over a long shooting weekend in the winter of 1896. It also, no doubt, helped that his duchess was a fabulously rich, pretty and charming American. Furthermore it is quite possible that a gentle word of support from Aunt Jennie, in her royal lover's ear, helped propel Sunny to the zenith of Edward's Court. Sadly, the entire pack of cards came tumbling down a few years later when the Marlboroughs separated, much to their royal sponsor's displeasure.

Sunny with medals and Garter c.1912. Like his monarch, Edward VII,
the patriotic Duke adhered strictly to protocol, had a weakness for
pageantry and thrilled to the pomp and circumstance of ancient tradition.

1902 was a momentous year in Sunny's life. On the face of it Sunny and Consuelo were the dazzling young couple at the new King's court. Consuelo had also been honoured by Queen Alexandra at the Coronation as she was selected as one of the four duchesses who were to be her canopy bearers during the ceremony. The gilded couple were driven to the Abbey in the crimson Marlborough state coach, the coachman adorned in:

> A beautiful livery of crimson cloth with silver braid on which were stamped the double-headed eagles of the Holy Roman Empire of which Marlborough was a Prince.

They were the toast of international society despite the fact that beneath the surface their marriage was on the rocks and Sunny had probably begun his long love affair with Gladys Deacon.

Foreign tours

January saw the Marlboroughs in Russia where they attended the great court functions which then ushered in the Orthodox New Year. They attended a fabulous ball at the Winter Palace where Consuelo, bedecked in diamonds, tiara and white satin, sat next to the Tsar, Nicholas II, and Sunny wore his Privy Councillor's uniform with white knee-breeches and

Consuelo at the Delhi Durbar.

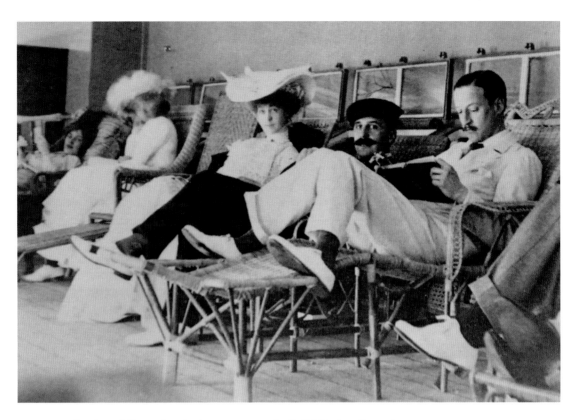

Sunny and Consuelo relaxing en route to the Delhi Durbar December 1902.

a blue coat embellished with gold lace, together with feathered hat under his arm. There were evenings at the ballet, excursions on open sleighs on the frozen Neva, suppers amongst the picture galleries of the Hermitage and grand dinners at the British Embassy to meet Russian society, including coveys of Grand Dukes and Duchesses. It was one enormous fairy tale that would tragically be terminated within a few years by the Russian Revolution.

In the late autumn Sunny and Consuelo set off with sixty other aristocratic friends for India to attend the Delhi Durbar as guests of Lord Curzon, the Viceroy.

The Durbar had been meticulously organised by the Viceroy to celebrate the succession of King Edward VII and Queen Alexandra as Emperor and Empress of India. The King could not attend owing to his illness and the Duke of Connaught was sent in his place. A deserted plain was turned into a tented city complete with its own light railway. The ceremony took place on New Year's Day 1903 with the massed ranks of the Indian Army under Lord Kitchener on parade with their regimental

The elephant procession at the Delhi Durbar. Consuelo wrote 'From the moment of our arrival in Bombay where Marlborough and I were guests of the governor, events as glamorous and gorgeous as those narrated in the tails of The Arabian Nights, enchanted us.

bands. Maharajahs came from all over India completing the display of the greatest collection of jewels ever supposedly seen in one location. This was the British Empire at its pinnacle. How Sunny must have adored the pomp and splendour of it all, Consuelo would later write:

> From the moment of our arrival in Bombay, where Marlborough and I were guests of the Governor, events as glamorous and gorgeous as those narrated in the tales of *The Arabian Nights* enchanted us.

Under-Secretary of State for the Colonies

On his return from India in late February, ministerial promotion was not long in coming. On 22 July 1903 Sunny landed the glamorous job of Under-Secretary of State for the Colonies. It was one thing to occupy

The tented village at the Delhi Durbar.

the unobtrusive office of Paymaster General but quite another to become 'number two' to Joe Chamberlain who presided over the greatest Empire the world had ever witnessed. By the age of thirty Sunny had proved himself not only a highly resourceful, if unexciting, government minister but also a staunch and dedicated member of the Conservative Party. Sunny's busy political schedule meant spending the week in London away from Blenheim where the land agent was left in charge. Luckily, the Marlboroughs' new London residence, Sunderland House, was completed in 1902 as Consuelo found herself entertaining numerous foreign dignitaries. Sunderland House, located at the top end of Curzon Street near Shepherd's Market, was designed by French architect, Achille Duchêne, and was a gift from Consuelo's father, William K. Vanderbilt.

Back in August 1901, Sunny hosted an extravagant political rally at Blenheim to celebrate the alliance between Salisbury's Conservatives and Chamberlain's Liberal Unionists. At his own expense, Sunny gave luncheon to 3,000 delegates from across the country, in addition to over 100 Members of Parliament. In the afternoon the Park was opened to the general public and the crowds in the Palace courtyard swelled to over 7,000. It would have been unlikely for such generosity and wholesome moral support to go unnoticed by the party leadership particularly as both his future chiefs were presiding over this magnificent gala. The

Sunny speaking at the second great Conservative and Unionist rally at Blenheim in 1908.
He is sharing the platform with his lifelong friend, the brilliant F.E.Smith, made Baron
Birkenhead in 1919, Viscount in 1921 and Earl in 1922.

following year, Arthur Balfour would succeed his uncle, Lord Salisbury
as leader of the Conservative Party.

Patronage may also have played a part in Sunny's promotion. Balfour
was a frequent guest at Blenheim and became a close friend of the duchess. Consuelo writes in *The Glitter and the Gold*:

> Balfour became one of my truest friends, a friendship I remember with
> humility and gratitude, for there has I believe, never been anybody quite
> like him. When I think of him it is as some fine and disembodied spirit.
> The opinions he expressed and the doctrines he held seemed to me to be
> the products of pure logic. Invariably he sensed the heart of the matter
> and freed it of sordid encumbrance and when he spoke in a philosophic
> vein it was like listening to Bach. His way of holding his head gave him
> the appearance of searching the heavens and his blue eyes were absent,
> and yet intent, as if busy in some abstract world.

The Prime Minister A.J. Balfour who gave Sunny his first big job as Under-Secretary of State for the Colonies. Consuelo wrote, 'Balfour became one of my truest friends, a friendship I remember with humility and gratitude, for there has, I believe, never been anybody quite like him.'

Balfour had a penchant for free-minded, intelligent and beautiful women and this could only work to Sunny's advantage.

Being a Parliamentary Under-Secretary can at the best of times be a frustrating appointment. Most Secretaries of State are too selfish and ambitious to allow their juniors much credit. The job entails making oneself as useful as possible to ones chief. It was bad enough working under a forceful superior in the Commons but one was all the more obscure being buried away in the Lords. It can be speculated that Sunny had a testing time working for one of Britain's most distinguished Edwardian politicians, Joe Chamberlain. Interestingly, Sunny's predicament was the complete antithesis of his successor, Winston. After the Liberal election landslide of December 1905, Winston turned down the prestigious post of working under Asquith at the Treasury to accept the junior ministerial post at the

Colonies. Why? Not because he was taking over from his cousin Sunny but rather because the new Secretary of State for the Colonies, Lord Elgin, was in the Lords, had little interest in politics, disliked giving speeches and kept his head down in Cabinet. Winston assumed he could run rings around him and at the same time achieve a prominent position in the Commons following Chamberlain as spokesman on colonial affairs.

Imperial Preference

Having said all this, the summer of 1903 was an exciting time for Sunny to join Chamberlain at the Colonial Office. On 15 May, in his West Birmingham constituency, Joe Chamberlain gave what must surely be the most sensational speech in British political history; ironically it would have far reaching consequences for Sunny. The heart of the message was that the Empire was in danger of disintegrating. His answer was to impose closer economic ties. He would introduce a system of protective tariffs on goods imported from outside the Empire to regenerate imperial ties. The adverse side of such action meant higher prices for basic foodstuffs as tariffs were placed on American bread or Argentinian beef. This was political dynamite as many people felt that Britain's greatness was built on free trade.

The issue of free trade would complete the unification of the Liberal Party and split the Conservative and Liberal Unionist Party down the middle. Balfour, the detached intellectual, refused to come down one side or the other and was increasingly seen as a weak and wounded Prime Minister. As the Cabinet failed to agree on a united policy, Chamberlain resigned in September, to be followed by two senior free trade ministers: Charles Ritchie, Chancellor of the Exchequer, and the Duke of Devonshire. Margot Asquith recorded in her autobiography that following the resignations her husband came into her bedroom at 20 Cavendish Square waving a copy of *The Times* saying: 'Wonderful news today, it is only a matter of time when we will sweep the country'. The Liberal election landslide would, in the event, be another two years in coming and with it Sunny would lose his job, ironically, to his cousin Winston. In due course, and in Sunny's view far worse than Imperial Preference, the Liberal Government would push through the Parliament Act, emasculating the power of the House of Lords and thereby ending hundreds of years of rule by the aristocracy.

Joe Chamberlain, Sunny's chief at the Colonial Office, resigned in September 1903 over 'Imperial Preference' and was replaced by Alfred Lyttelton.

In 1903, following the resignation of Chamberlain, Sunny had a new chief at the Colonial Office. Alfred Lyttelton, who had been the Liberal Unionist Member of Parliament for Warwick and Leamington since 1895 and was a celebrated athlete and socialite, having represented England at cricket and football. He married Laura Tennant, Margo Asquith's sister. One must assume that the two men were known to each other before working together in Office, as Lyttelton was one of a small group of M.P.s who were both socially and politically prominent. Lyttelton would famously say of the ambitious Winston when he crossed the floor of the House: 'One might as well try and rebuke a brass band, he trims his sails to every passing wind.'

As a junior minister at the Colonial Office Sunny had to answer questions in the Lords on many mundane matters such as freight rates to the colonies, overseas emigration statistics, the ballasting of ships, salvage claims, life-saving apparatus on ships and administrative details in connection with the Colonial Conference of 1907. But he also faced the intellectually demanding task of defending the government's stance on Imperial Preference. This was no easy brief as the views of Balfour and Chamberlain more often than not were diametrically opposed and as a result the Prime Minister stubbornly refused to come off the fence. The whole issue of Tariff Reform was a complicated issue and on 20 July 1905 Sunny had to reply to the Duke of Devonshire's motion as to the differing policies of Chamberlain and Balfour in connection with Food Taxes and confirm whether Balfour was still Prime Minister. Sunny 'ducked and weaved' successfully and explained that all coalitions had to live with differing opinions whether it be the Radicals and the newly formed Labour Party or the Liberals and the Irish Party. He insisted that the government would not be rushed into establishing any closer commercial ties with the colonies, and indeed, express any definite policies until they had heard the views of the participants at the forthcoming Colonial Conference.

Native labourers in the Transvaal
Another highly controversial area where Sunny and Winston found themselves on different sides of the fence at this time was over the issue of ill treatment of native labourers in the Transvaal gold mines. Owing to appalling working conditions mortality in the mines had risen to 80 per 1,000; twenty times worse than in the British coalfields. Coupled with low wages and harsh discipline it was becoming increasingly difficult for mine owners to recruit new workers. As a result the Conservative Government had agreed to the importation of contracted Chinese labour. When certain mine owners were accused of illegally flogging some of their workers in their compounds, the Liberal Party, with the support of wavering Tories, Winston and Jack Seely, launched a crusade against such recruitment practices, accusing the government of reintroducing slavery in the process.

On 21 March 1904 when Seely spoke in support of Liberal leader, Henry Campbell-Bannerman's motion of censure on the issue, he was greeted with such an uproar from the Conservative benches that he was unable to make himself heard. Winston rose to defend his good friend and stated: 'I am quite unable to hear what my honourable friend is saying owing to the vulgar clamour maintained by the Conservative Party.' By the end of May both men had crossed the floor of the House to the Liberal benches. On 20 June Sunny had the unenviable task of defending the government's position in the Lords. Along with Food Taxes, the Chinese labour question would become the main issue in the December 1905 Election campaign when the Liberals won their landslide victory leaving Sunny out of office for over a decade.

Operating at the Colonial Office

A newspaper cutting dated 31 August 1918, discovered in one of Glady's letters, gives a fascinating account of Sunny's modus operandi at the Colonial Office through the eyes of F.G.A. Butler, his private secretary:

> The Duke is one of the most modest and moderate of men, and, unlike most of his predecessors at the Colonial Office, he insisted on doing some work not only in the office but also at home. All the permanent heads of the office who did likewise were in the habit of sending the official papers to their private houses in dispatch boxes and pouches by messengers specially retained for this duty. The Duke of Marlborough to the consternation of the messengers insisted on carrying home his own boxes and pouches and as he walked across Horse Guards Parade ground with a pouch or two in each hand he looked more unlike a Duke than a light porter.

In sharp contrast Winston's watch at the Colonial Office proved to be characteristically exhausting:

> When the Duke was succeeded by his cousin, Mr Winston Churchill in 1905, the newcomer would have none of the mild and meticulous methods of his kinsman. Minutes and dispatches were dashed off with lightning rapidity, rules and regulations which, for ages before, had safely and efficiently governed the conduct of official business were either ruthlessly revoked or moulded anew. The whole department, in fact, became electrified, the mark-time methods of the permanent staff were changed into full gallop, even poor Lord Elgin, the Secretary of State, was left hopelessly

panting in the rear. At length Mr Churchill was promoted to the Board of Trade, the staff wiped their streaming foreheads, and, after a decent interval of mental and physical response, resumed their former ways.

Out of office

In his years out of office Sunny regularly attended the House of Lords, often speaking on agricultural matters. On 25 November 1915 he spoke in the House of Lords expressing concern at the government's plans to enlist 60,000 agricultural labourers. He stated that this proposed action would have a grave impact on the production of food. If this took place he concluded that:

> Steps ought to be taken to organise female labour for agricultural purposes and women should be made to realise that if they offered their services for work of that kind they were helping to win the war just as much as were men in the trenches.

On 28 February 1916 the Women's National Land Service Corps was founded with Sunny as its President. At its inaugural meeting a week later at the Grosvenor House in London he told the audience that 'if he could make do with young boys, old men and women on his farms then others could as well.'

Under-Secretary at Agriculture and Fisheries

Arguably the most surprising ministerial appointment of Sunny's career was that of joint Under-Secretary at Agriculture and Fisheries in the summer of 1917. Sunny's one-time 'great enemy', Lloyd George had ousted Asquith in 1916 and was now heading up his own Coalition Government. Sunny detested Lloyd George's past radicalism, his introduction of 'the People's Budget' which raised taxes on the rich and the imposition of the Parliament Act abolishing the House of Lord's power of veto. He considered the Welshman's shrill speeches, attacking the aristocracy, divisive and distasteful, particularly the Limehouse speech in 1909 directed specifically at the Dukes.

So why was Sunny offered a ministerial post in the Coalition Government led by Lloyd George? Firstly we must assume that Sunny was considered a capable candidate. His abilities were obviously well respected

A scene straight out of a Thomas Hardy novel? Sunny and Gladys at the Blenheim sheep sales c1922. Sunny's ministerial career was resurrected with his inclusion in the Lloyd George government as Under-Secretary of State for Agriculture and Fisheries, where he proved a knowledgeable and assiduous minister.

in high places and agriculture was after all 'his special subject'. But perhaps Lloyd George, now Prime Minister in a Coalition Government, was trying to heal old wounds? In the summer of 1917 he brought Winston back in from the wilderness as Minister of Munitions amidst much Conservative scepticism. He also held out the olive branch to Asquith offering him the Chancellorship which in this case was declined. So why not make his peace with the battered aristocracy in the process?

We must assume that Winston, for a decade now, extremely close to Lloyd George, made a strong case for bringing his cousin back into government. Violet Bonham Carter in her book on Winston, *As I Knew Him*, wrote:

> The inner citadel of the heart held first and foremost his relations – in
> their widest sense. His strong family feeling embraced not only his mother
> and his brother, Jack, but cousins, uncles, aunts – the whole Guest tribe
> and Sunny, Duke of Marlborough. (He confided to me that one of the

reasons for preferring the post of Colonial Under-Secretary to that of Financial Secretary to the Treasury was that Sunny had once held it.) I often told him that one quality he shared with his great hero Napoleon was nepotism; that if he had been Napoleon he would have popped all the Guests, his brother Jack, and Sunny Marlborough on every throne in Europe and made his mother Empress of Byzantium. He did not deny it and suggested, 'It might have been quite a good thing to do. I think Sunny would have done very well in Spain'.

In this case we must assume that Winston's nepotism proved an asset to his country as Sunny proved an assiduous Under-Secretary. Between May and July 1917, amongst other matters, Sunny spoke on the following topics; the employment of prisoners of war, the increased cultivation of arable land, ploughing up grasslands, the provision of labour, horses, machinery and refrigeration plants, the provision of seeds and fertiliser, proposals for the establishment of a Wages Board, milk supply and food shortages, controlling the supply of fish, salmon fishing and the environmental condition of the country's rivers.

If Sunny disliked Lloyd George as much as we are led to believe, then why did he accept a position in his Coalition Government? As mentioned above, agriculture was his speciality and he felt he could make a worthwhile contribution. Moreover, he was coming back into mainstream politics alongside his close cousin, Winston, who no doubt had furthered his cause with the Prime Minister. Most importantly, however, was that Sunny was a true patriot. He had served as a King's Messenger, taking important documents to France in the early years of the war and now his eldest son, Bert was being sent to the Front to fight. In the intervening years he had played a large part in forming the Women's Land Army in addition to placing Blenheim on a war footing. He turned the Long Library into a military hospital, donated a herd of beef cattle to the nation, grew cabbages in his herbaceous borders, converted the Estate timber mill at Combe for war production and ploughed up the sheep walks in the Park. It was only natural that he would want to serve his country. What better way for a middle aged man of forty-six to achieve that goal than by participating in his country's governances.

7

Cousins make the best friends

Sunny Marlborough was not only Winston Spencer-Churchill's close kinsman but also his best friend. On Monday 2 July 1934 the obituary columns of *The Times* newspaper carried a tribute to the 9th Duke of Marlborough by his first cousin, Winston commencing: 'I thought I might write a few lines about my oldest and dearest friend before he is carried to his tomb.' Likewise, Sunny regarded Winston as his closest confidant. In their early twenties the two cousins would act more like brothers and their friendship would remain strong and constant over the next forty years despite notorious family quarrels and glaring political differences. Roy Jenkins wrote in his biography on Churchill following the latter's exit from the Conservative Party in 1904:

> Much to his credit Marlborough never faltered during those years in his family loyalty or genuine friendship towards Churchill for whom Blenheim remained a safe and welcoming haven.

Blenheim played a paramount part in both cousins' lives. Winston once famously stated that he made the two most important decisions of his life at Blenheim, 'to be born and to be married'. Ironically, Sunny, who inherited the dukedom and Blenheim, was born at the hill station, Simla, in India and was engaged to be married when staying with the Vanderbilts in Newport, Rhode Island. Both men had a deep inbuilt sense of duty. Sunny served his country, both politically and militarily, early in his career before immersing himself in the heavy responsibilities of transforming the Palace

The four cousins at the Queen's Own Oxfordshire Hussars summer camp. From left to right sitting Sunny, Viscount Churchill standing and wearing a dark uniform, Winston Churchill standing with his hand on his brother's shoulder, Jack Churchill sitting on the right.

and its surrounding Park into the glorious World Heritage Centre we witness today. He sacrificed his personal happiness to secure the necessary funding for his predestined task whereas Winston contracted a happy marriage at Blenheim that would form the bedrock of a unique political career.

Childhood friendship

During their childhood the two cousins saw little of each other. Their respective fathers, Lord Blandford and Lord Randolph Spencer-Churchill,

Lilian Hammersley, the second wife of the 8th Duke of Marlborough, who was popular with both Sunny and Winston.

had grown apart following the breach over the Aylesford affair, a public scandal that involved the Spencer-Churchill family and the Prince of Wales. There was a brief respite in the summer of 1883 on the death of their grandfather, the 7th Duke, when occasional meetings took place at Blenheim and in London. On 9 September 1883, Lord Randolph wrote to his wife Jennie:

> I hope you had a nice time at Blenheim and that Winston was good. I think it is rather rash of you letting him be at Blenheim without you. I don't know who will look after him and Sunny.

Again in January 1885 Jennie almost apologetically writes to her husband about her sons Winston and Jack:

> They both went to tea with Sunny yesterday and they all met in the Park and Bertha [Albertha the 8th Duchess and a daughter of the Duke of

Abercorn] wrote and asked if they might come – so I let them.

The family feud was soon renewed when the 8th Duke decided to break up Blenheim's magnificent picture collection owing to many years of family profligacy. In 1888 the 8th Duke, a clever amateur scientist, remarried an American heiress, Lilian Hammersley, whose fortune went some way to restoring the Blenheim Estate. In addition to electric lighting, an early telephone system was installed in the Palace and improvements were made to the farming enterprises.

Winston made sporadic visits to Blenheim in his childhood to stay with his grandparents but rarely saw Sunny who was living with his mother, Albertha, at Oakdene in Surrey. On 1 April 1882 Winston wrote to his mother, Jennie, from Blenheim: 'The Gardens and the Park are so much nicer to walk in than Green Park or Hyde Park' and to his father, Randolph, a week later:

> Jack and I went to the Lince on Thursday and gathered a lot of wild hyacinths. When we were out on Friday near the Cascade we saw a snake crawling about in the grass. I wanted to kill it but Everest [Nanny] would not let me.

Winston's deep affection for Blenheim which he shared throughout his life with Sunny was formulated at an early age yet quite independently of his cousin who he evidently hardly knew by the time Sunny succeeded to the dukedom in November 1892.

Growing friendship
On the death of her husband Albertha returned to Blenheim to support her son, Sunny, in his elevated role. She was also determined to heal the wounds of the past and she invited Winston to Christmas the following year. True to form, Lord Randolph wrote grudgingly to his mother, Duchess Fanny about Winston:

> I do not mind his going to Blenheim as long as I don't go there myself. They seem to make a fuss with him and of course he knows nothing of the past.

The Saloon at Blenheim Palace 1896

Christmas 1893 proved a great success for Winston. Christmas night dinner in the Saloon, late night political discussion in the grand cabinet, lengthy walks in the gardens beside the lake on the way to the cascade, a Boxing Day shoot around the Park belts and best of all, because the cousins were excellent horsemen, riding in the old medieval park around High Lodge.

On Christmas Day Winston wrote to his mother:

> There is no sort of party and I am quite alone with Sunny. He is very good company and we have sat talking till 1.30am every night since I have been here.

It was the perfect opportunity for the two budding politicians to discover each other and dispel any misconceptions caused by bygone family feuds. Again, on 30 December, Winston wrote to Lady Randolph:

> Sunny has been very kind and we have had very lengthy conversations. It is most untrue to say he is stupid. He is very sensible and I think, clever – extremely industrious and attentive to business and he seems to have made himself very popular with the tenancy and neighbours.

In the same vein he wrote to his aunt, Leonie Leslie, on Boxing Day:

> Perhaps you will be astonished at the notepaper. Sunny very kindly asked me down here for the Christmas week. He is such an interesting companion and anything but the idiot I was taught to believe him to be.

Winston, in turn, obviously made a good impression on his cousin and in the New Year their relationship became stronger still, Winston writing to his father on 31 January 1894:

> Today I met Sunny in Hill Street – up for the Bass wedding. He was very amiable and took me to lunch at Whites where I met several people I had been at Harrow with.

And again, Albertha, writing to her nephew, Winston, on 19 March:

> Sunny hopes you will come to Blenheim for Easter.

Sunny and Winston were united at the outset of their relationship by proud family ties but they soon found themselves united by a shared interest in politics. When Sunny, as a young member of the House of Lords moved the Vote of Thanks in reply to the Loyal Address following the Queen's Speech, Winston, a newly joined subaltern in the 4th Hussars, wrote to, his mother, Jennie, on 16 August 1895, rather patronisingly and, perhaps, with a hint of jealousy:

> I do not care to dwell on the past but I could not help thinking as I read it that Papa would like to see that Sunny had inherited at least some of the family talents and was trying quietly and tactfully to use them. I wonder whether he will have the self-control to relapse for a little longer into silence.

Surely this is a little rich coming from Winston! From the tender age of twenty-one Winston had a yearning to follow his elder cousin into politics, remarking to his mother: 'It is a fine game to play – the game of politics – and it is well worth waiting for a good hand before really plunging'. Unlike Sunny, Winston did not have a ready entré into politics or the opportunity to 'polish his mind' over three years at Cambridge, so he resolved to educate himself through copious reading while away on service in India.

The friendship between the two cousins developed through written correspondence while Winston was in India. In 1898 he wrote to Sunny:

> My dear, I hesitate how to begin. Sunny, though melodious sounds child-ish: Marlborough is very formal: Duke impossible between relations: and I don't suppose you answer to either Charles or Richard. If I must reflect let it be Sunny. But you must perceive in all this a strong case for the abolition of the House of Lords and all titles. [1]

The latter sentence points to the beginning of a widening political divide between the cousins caused by Winston's developing reactionary views. Sunny was by birth a Conservative, and Winston, the product of a second son, would soon join the ranks of the radical Liberals.

On 6 November 1895 Sunny married Consuelo Vanderbilt, one of the world's richest heiresses, in New York. To all intents and purposes it was an arranged marriage. Ever since he was a boy Sunny had been constantly reminded by his grandmother, Duchess Fanny, that Blenheim was financially strained and he needed to marry for money. Consuelo's mother Alva was a pushy society hostess and was deeply ambitious for her daughter. Only an English Duke complete with his own palace was good enough for Consuelo. Winston surprisingly missed the wedding arriving in New York three days later as he had been detained in Cuba, where having embarked on his career in journalism, he was covering the Cuban War of Independence. Ivor Guest, (later Viscount Wimborne) another first cousin and a close friend at Cambridge, was best man. On 15 November Winston wrote to his brother, Jack:

> I saw Sunny last night and am dining with the Vanderbilts this evening. He is very pleased with himself and seems very fit. The newspapers have

abused him scurrilously. But the essence of American journalism is vulgarity divested of truth.

By their late twenties the respect and friendship between the two cousins had seemingly become strong enough to enable Winston to have the confidence to seek financial assistance from Sunny. Owing to the delicate state of her finances, Jennie Churchill was finding it difficult to pay her sons their annual allowances, £500 to Winston and £200 to his younger brother, Jack. Winston wrote to Sunny asking him if he would be willing to guarantee a loan he was trying to raise on behalf of his mother to assist providing the allowances. On 7 July 1898 while travelling from India to join Kitchener's campaign on the Nile, Winston wrote to Sunny:

> If you will assist I should be very much obliged to you and shall not easily forget an act of kindness. If not – the fact of my putting this in writing will make it easy for you to refuse without embarrassment and the refusal will I hope make no difference to the friendship and affection which exists between us.

Presumably there was a happy outcome, for Winston wrote to his mother a few months later from Cairo:

> I had a long letter from Marlborough just before I left India. He has been and will, I hope, continue to be a very good friend to me.

In August 1900 Winston was back at Blenheim writing to Jennie:

> We had speeches here yesterday to a Primrose League meeting – Sunny, Ivor and I – rather interesting. Sunny speaks so well. I was very impressed.

Sunny was certainly a competent performer with a prepared speech but he was not an instinctive debater. He did not have the confidence or showmanship of Randolph and Winston. He was not 'quick on his feet' writing to Winston a few years later:

> I thank you for your kind letter. I was very dissatisfied with my performance this evening. I possess no readiness of resource and on thinking

Sunny on his favourite 'Blenheim Grey', Evenlode, by Munnings with Lord Ivor, his second son, to the right of the picture.

out points afterwards I realise how many good arguments I let slip. The army analogy at which they laughed was badly presented by me, and I ought to have stopped and taken the other side up on their merriment. But I lack the confidence.

It was not only politics they had in common. A month later Winston was again writing to his mother: 'I had a very pleasant time in Paris. Sunny and I had long talks about all kinds of things.' The following year Sunny asked Winston to join him for a few days hunting in Leicestershire where he owned a hunting lodge at Sysonby near Melton Mowbray. Twenty grey hunters were kept at the home farm in Bladon on the Blenheim Estate and administered by a staff of a dozen, the whole entourage being conveyed by special train from Woodstock to Melton. Sunny was a brilliant horseman and hunted with the Quorn in Leicestershire, the Pytchley in Northamptonshire and closer to home with the Bicester. After his death Winston wrote:

> I admired him with his light weight and fine grey horses, when I often, from amid the crowd or around the gates or the gaps, saw him two or three fields to the right or to the left of the hunt, sailing over the big fences which none of us had touched before and where none followed after.

At around the same time Consuelo was writing to Gladys Deacon, who would become Sunny's second wife in 1920: 'Sunny is still devoutly attentive to Winston's every remark – a great sign of friendship', and perhaps, more tellingly, she recounts: 'Winston is still on the talk – never stops and really becomes tiring'. A lifelong friendship would develop despite Winston's exhausting and contrasting personality. Perhaps Sunny was slightly in awe of his cousin's growing eloquence, energy and fortitude?

Mutual respect

Winston had come to respect Sunny's judgement and would often seek his advice. Following the relief of Khartoum, Kitchener confronted a French expedition on the upper reaches of the Nile which nearly caused war between the two countries. Winston wrote to his mother:

> I enclose a letter about my article on the Fashoda Incident – will you show it to Sunny or send it to him with just a line to say I asked you to.

For his part, Sunny was proud of Winston's literary and political aspirations. The Duke was determined to support his cousin's quest for a parliamentary seat, not only giving him £400 towards his September 1900 election expenses, but also generously handing over to him the unexpired two years of a lease he held on a flat at 105 Mount Street in Mayfair. Winston in turn was sensitive in his dealings with his highly-strung cousin. In March 1898 the first of Winston's many books, *The Story of the Malakand Field Force* was published receiving stellar reviews. An immediate result of its success was a series of invitations from publishers to write articles and books. One such request was to write a life of the 1st Duke of Marlborough which Winston declined as he did not wish to trespass on Sunny's territory.

Sunny, Winston and Jack were loyal members of the Queen's Own Oxfordshire Hussars (also known as the Oxfordshire Yeomanry). Sunny sits in the middle on a large chair. Jack is at the far left of the middle row sitting next to his brother, Winston, who wears a hat with a white cloth attached covering his neck.

By the turn of the century Sunny had become both mentor and sounding board for his cousin's blossoming political career. On 14 July 1898 Winston made his first major political speech when he spoke for fifty-five minutes at a public meeting in Bradford. He wrote euphorically to Sunny: 'Bradford was the greatest pleasure of my life, I hope to have more…' In June 1899 during his unsuccessful General Election campaign in Oldham, he told his cousin: 'I am getting on very well and scoring off all the people who ask me questions', and again just before polling:

> My private impression is that we shall be beaten in spite of Mawdsley, (the very competent Conservative working class candidate) and in spite of everything I can do, and we shall be beaten simply because the Government have brought forward this stupid Bill which can do them no possible good.[2]

The following year, immediately before the October Election, when Winston was elected for Oldham, Sunny accompanied him both on a trip to Paris to view the International Exhibition and on a countrywide

A weekend house party at Blenheim Palace in the 1920s. F.E.Smith and Winston sit on the far left on the base of the pillar. Sunny stands on the far right at the top of the steps, wearing a white suit.

speaking tour which included an invitation to speak on behalf of their cousin, Ivor Guest, in Plymouth.

If lifelong friendships are forged at university, similar youthful bonding must surely be cemented during time spent in the armed services, particularly in a wartime environment. Sunny was a commissioned lieutenant in his yeomanry regiment, the Queen's Own Oxfordshire Hussars in 1894. With his cousin, Winston, he would enjoy many high-spirited summer camps in Blenheim Park before the First World War. Michael Sheldon in his book *Young Titan* noted:

> There were memorable nights when Sunny Marlborough, Winston and a
> few other friends would gather in a field tent and sit on upturned barrels,
> by the light of tallow candles playing cards until the flush of dawn.

Among those close friends was the brilliant F.E. Smith who would become the youngest Lord Chancellor since Judge Jeffreys in the 1680s.

A Boxing Day meet at Blenheim Palace with F.E. Smith's wife and Clementine Churchill standing next to Sunny, who is in the middle at the back. F.E. Smith stands on the far right with a cigar in his mouth. The future 10th Duke of Marlborough, and grandfather of Michael Waterhouse, stands in front of his father.

F.E. was born in 1877 and went up to Wadham College, Oxford where he read law and distinguished himself in the Oxford Union. Politically, he and Sunny were well matched, both being staunch Conservatives, yet the two men came from opposite backgrounds. The Smiths had been miners, schoolmasters and solicitors from the north of England and F.E. would continue the family tradition of self-betterment in expansive style. F.E. lived in the north of the county at Charlton, a 12 mile horse ride from Blenheim. John Campbell in his biography of F.E. Smith commented:

> The serious military purpose of these camps was minimal – they simply enjoyed the opportunity to ride around in uniform with their friends. The evenings were given over to conversation or cards. It was at one of these Blenheim camps that F.E., playing against Sunny, their host, was asked what they should play for. 'Your bloody palace if you like', he replied.

Sunny not only enjoyed F.E.'s sense of humour but also his intellect, his brilliant conversational abilities and his bravery as a horseman. Winston also came to love this exciting, hard drinking, high living politician and the three men would become life-long friends spending many a happy Christmas together at Blenheim. Randolph Churchill remembers one special Blenheim Christmas when there was a double celebration to mark both the end of the First World War and Lord Blandford's coming of age:

> There was a paper chase on horseback and a whole ox was roasted. The day concluded with a gigantic bonfire on top of which was placed an effigy of the Kaiser. I seem to remember that F.E.'s daughter, Lady Eleanor Smith, contributed a discarded pair of stockings which were stuffed with straw and served as the Imperial legs.

Freddy Birkenhead, F.E.'s son, recalls his childhood memories of these magical family Christmases at Blenheim writing:

> Every aspect filled us with excitement and invited exploration. The Great Hall with its radiators on which we lay on our backs and gazed at the painted ceiling, the Long Library and the Willis Organ, strewn around this great room were white bear skin rugs on which we lay while, Perkins, the organist, indifferent to the political arguments of the adults and the noise of the children, sat by the hour immersed in his own world, playing Bach fugues and improvising themes.

In a similar vein his sister, Lady Eleanor Smith wrote:

> Christmas at Blenheim was something to be remembered all year long. Guests would have tea in the boathouse by the Lake and the Blue Hungarian Band came from London to play for dinner – no expense spared. Torchlight processions were held in the Park and through the streets of the town and it was not uncommon to roast a whole ox.

Sunny and Winston would soon be united once again, this time in war-torn South Africa in 1900. An uneasy balance between the Boer and British populations in South Africa had been upset by the gold rush of the 1880's. The British immigrant miners (Uitlanders) were refused voting and other rights causing the tension between the Boer Republics to increase until war broke out in 1899. Needless to say, the swashbuckling Winston sailed immediately for Cape Town as principal war correspondent for the *Morning Post*. In November he was captured by the Boers, following the celebrated armoured train incident. He subsequently escaped, thereby achieving his much sought-after heroic fame which shortly afterwards launched his political career. Sunny, now a Staff Captain in the Imperial Yeomanry, arrived in South Africa for very different reasons early in 1900. He was endeavouring to escape from a failing marriage to Consuelo.

Until Sunny teamed up with Winston he had experienced little front line action as he was attached to Lord Roberts' headquarters staff along with two other dukes, Norfolk and Westminster. In Britain, the radical press mocked this ducal assemblage which was seen to be shirking the firing-line. The Commander-in-Chief was, therefore, more than pleased when Winston suggested that his cousin join him as part of Ian Hamilton's

The boathouse next to the Lake at Blenheim, built by the 8th Duke with Lilian Hammersley's money.

column for the march on Pretoria. Randolph Churchill remarked in his biography of his father:

> For this expedition Churchill had equipped himself and Marlborough with a wagon and a team of four horses. There was a false bottom to the wagon in which were installed the best-tinned provisions and alcoholic stimulants which London could supply.

Winston himself wrote to his mother on 1 May 1900 from Bloemfontein:

> Marlborough and I are just starting to join General Hamilton's column, some forty miles away from the railway line and hope from this quarter to cooperate in the general movement upon Kroonstad. It is very pleasant travelling with him.

On the same day Winston wrote to his brother Jack:

> Marlborough is here and I saw a great deal of Ivor Guest during a rather interesting little operation we had in the right hand corner of the Orange Free State.

This wartime experience gave all three cousins the opportunity to discover each other in much the same way as Sunny and Ivor had bonded at Cambridge. In June, Winston wrote to his mother: 'Sunny is very keen and he and I have listened to a good many bullets and shells together.' Winston later described their entry into the Boer capital in *My Early Life:*

> Early on the morning of June 5th Marlborough and I rode out together and soon reached the head of an infantry column already in the outskirts of town. There were no military precautions and we arrived, a large group of officers, at the closed gates of the railway crossing. Quite slowly, there now steamed past before our eyes, a long train, drawn by two engines and crammed with armed Boers, whose rifles bristled from every window. We gazed at each other dumbfounded at three yards distance. A single shot would have precipitated a horrible carnage on both sides. Although sorry that the train should escape, it was with unfeigned relief that we saw the last carriage glide slowly past our noses. Then

A portrait of Sunny in Imperial Yeomanry Uniform during the Boer War. On the back of this portrait the following is written:- Charles, Richard, John, Spencer Churchill, Duke of Marlborough Capetown 1900. Zand River, Affair of Lindley, Engagement of Johannesburg, Engagement of Pretoria, Battle of Diamond Hill Jun 11th & 12th.

Marlborough and I cantered into town. We knew the officer prisoners had been removed from the State Model Schools, and we asked our way to the new cage where it was hoped they were still confined. We feared they had been carried off – perhaps in the very last train. But as we rounded a corner, there was the prison camp, a long tin building surrounded by a dense wire entanglement. I raised my hat and cheered. The cry was instantly answered from within. What followed resembled the end of an Adelphi melodrama. We were only two, and before us stood the armed Boer guards with their rifles at the ready. Marlborough, resplendent in the red tabs of the Staff, called on the Commandant to surrender forthwith, adding by a happy thought that he would give a receipt for the rifles. The prisoners rushed out of the house into the yard, some in uniform, some in flannels, hatless or coatless, but all violently excited. The sentries threw down their rifles, the gates were flung open, and while the last of the guard (there were 52 in all) stood uncertain what to do, the penned-up officers surrounded them and seized their weapons. Someone produced a Union Jack, the Transvaal emblem was torn down and amidst wild cheers from our captive friends the first British flag was hoisted over Pretoria.

Sunny was mentioned in dispatches and the following year promoted to the rank of Major.

By mid-summer both cousins were back in London intent on furthering their political careers. Most urgently, they were needed to officiate at Jennie Churchill's wedding to George Cornwallis-West but Winston, always mindful of the need to make a living, was also keen to develop a literary reputation alongside his political aspirations. Thanks to Sunny's generosity, Winston would soon receive celebrity status with the publication of his biography on his father, Lord Randolph. Between 1902 and October 1905, Winston produced a two-volume, 250,000 word book based on painstaking personal research, mostly undertaken at Blenheim. During this period the two cousins became closer still as Sunny provided shelter and sustenance at the Palace for the author. Randolph Churchill writes of Sunny's benevolence in his biography of his father, Winston:

> It is one of the merits of primogeniture that the money and amenities of a great family can be made available to gifted but impoverished members of a cadet branch. Thus it was that Churchill's cousin, Sunny Marlborough, placed a set of rooms at his disposal at Blenheim and mounted him on his fine hunters for three or four months during the years when he was writing his father's life. He also made Churchill free of the Muniment Room at Blenheim and subsequently caused all of Lord Randolph's important political papers to be bound in thirty-two handsome blue morocco

A portrait of Sunny by Umberto Veruda. With his slight stature and excellent balance Sunny was an accomplished horseman.

volumes, richly emblazoned back and front with the Marlborough arms in gold leaf.

Family loyalty was one of Sunny's most captivating attributes. When the *Daily Telegraph* published a scathing review of the biography, including an attack on Lord Randolph's character, Sunny wasted no time in leaping to his uncle's defence. On 3rd January 1906 he wrote to the editor:

> It is on behalf of Lord Randolph's family who loved him, his friends who esteemed him and his political associates who honoured him that I desire to offer an uncompromising protest against an attack on the memory of a departed statesman the method of which appears to me to be essentially un-English.

The use of the latter word refers not only to the fact that Lord Randolph was not alive to defend himself but less attractively it represented a dig at the Jewish ownership of the newspaper. The English aristocracy at the turn of the twentieth century was vigorously anti-Semitic.

Although Winston was beginning to make a useful living from his writing, money worries were always at the forefront of his mind and Sunny was not afraid to remind him of his fiscal responsibilities. The two cousins were united in a love of foxhunting with Sunny invariably the generous host. In November 1901 Sunny wrote to Winston suggesting he sold his hunters which he was allowed to stable at Blenheim:

> It occurs to me that you attempt too many things at the same moment. I am sorry your horses will be unused for so long. Hunting is expensive and is economical in proportion to the number of days that one hunts. If you do not mean to hunt until February, Wright [the Blenheim groom] urges you selling now at Leicester and hiring when you come home.

Whatever the outcome they continued to hunt together, for in December 1905, concerned for Winston's health and the fact that 'he was over-doing it', Sunny wrote:

> My dear, I was much concerned to see that you were unwell. Is it CB's [Campbell-Bannerman's] speeches, old D's bad champagne or the effects

of too frequent visits to the vicinity of Marshall and Snelgrove? Whatever the cause may be, I am concerned as to the result and I beg you to take life easy. I am bored here hunting alone.

The personal favours worked both ways. As Winston acquired more political influence he never forgot his cousin and was constantly pushing him forward for public office of sorts. In September 1902 he wrote to Joe Chamberlain:

> Have you ever considered Marlborough as a possible candidate for the post of Australian Governor-General. If he were asked – I think he would go. Blenheim would be a great sacrifice but on the other hand to have held such an office with credit for three or four years confers a permanent rank in the Imperial hierarchy.

Again, in August 1906, when it was proposed to set up a Royal Commission on the subject of reducing the high freight rates to South Africa, Winston wrote to the King:

> The President of the Board of Trade has thought of asking the Duke of Marlborough to become chairman of the Commission but I do not know whether he will accept.

Sunny was always mindful of his massive responsibilities, not least his grandiose improvement plans, at Blenheim.

Political split
As with so many families across the country Sunny's big political split with Winston came in the summer of 1903 over Tariff Reform. In mid-July Joe Chamberlain made a speech in Birmingham Town Hall that would radically change the course of British politics. The heart of his message was that the Empire was in danger of disintegrating unless held together economically. This necessitated the introduction of tariffs on goods imported from outside the Empire, such as American wheat. The effects which would push up the price of bread were political dynamite. The controversy that followed unified the Liberal Party and split the Conservatives and Liberal Unionists down the middle. In 1904 this split

led Winston and his cousin, Ivor Guest, to cross the floor of the House and join the Liberal Party. On 30 June 1903 Sunny wrote to Winston:

> I am sorrowful to think that we are at the parting of our political ways and I am grieved to feel that you are going to take such an aggressive part in opposition to the fiscal proposals of Balfour and Chamberlain. It will mean your ultimate severance from the Tory Party and your identification with Rosebery and his followers. I deplore the hasty position you have taken up however I will not pursue a topic further over which it is impossible for us ever to agree upon.

Their personal friendship was by now strong enough to weather the political storm, Winston writing to his mother on 12 August:

> Sunny is extremely pleased with his appointment. [Under-Secretary of State for the Colonies] He made an extremely good speech in the House of Lords on the Sugar Convention and everyone is loud in his praise. What a difference it makes to a man to get the 'claque' on his side. I see a great deal of him now and our relations are most cordial. [3]

Indeed, Consuelo writes in her autobiography:

> Marlborough's affection for his favourite cousins was in no way affected by their political views which were freely discussed around the dinner table, at which we often lingered until midnight, carried away by Winston's eloquence and by the equally brilliant and sophisticated defence of Conservatism offered by Hugh Cecil.

In October 1906 the Marlboroughs' marriage finally fell apart and Consuelo went to live at Sunderland House in Mayfair. The union had been a disaster from the start as neither party had been in love and they had quickly grown to dislike each other. After eleven years of marriage both parties had been unfaithful to each other. Although Consuelo was almost certainly the first to stray, she not only found Sunny impossible to live with but also hated the stuffy pomposity of aristocratic life in England. According to Sunny's friend, Hugh Cecil, the Duke had antediluvian views such as, 'Consuelo is unfit to live with as she went wrong before

Consuelo and Winston on the steps of Blenheim Palace. They became lifelong friends.

I did and because the standard for women in these things is higher than for men.'

Consuelo was indeed on weak ground as Edwardian divorce law favoured the male, as a husband could simply accuse his wife of infidelity while a wife had to prove both infidelity and physical cruelty. She was also making many visits to Paris, ostensibly to stay with her father, but in 1906 she was conducting a less than discreet affair with Sunny's cousin, Lord Castlereagh, the Conservative Member of Parliament for Maidstone and the eldest son of the formidable society hostess Lady Londonderry. Sunny, for his part, was taking a terrific pounding on the other side of the Atlantic from the American press that typecast him as the wicked

English Duke who married the young American heiress for her money. Into this maelstrom walked Winston as the chief intermediary.

Nobody wanted the Marlborough split to end up in court, particularly Winston and Castlereagh who had their political careers to think about. The publicity would reflect badly on society as a whole where the watchword was discretion. Winston and Consuelo had become close friends since her arrival in England. They had much in common; she, with her liberal American outlook, and he, with his radical politics coupled with an attractive youthful energy. It all provided a sharp contrast to Sunny's rather pompous, old-fashioned, conventional approach to life. Consuelo wrote of Winston in *The Glitter and the Gold*:

> Whether it was his American blood, his boyish enthusiasm and spontaneity, qualities sadly lacking in my husband, I delighted in his companionship. His conversation was invariably stimulating and his views on life were not drawn and quartered, as were Marlborough's by a sense of self-importance. To me he represented the democratic spirit so foreign to my environment and which I deeply missed.

Winston found himself in an uneasy position, caught between differing loyalties. He immediately championed his American soulmate, writing to his mother on 13 October 1906:

> Sunny has definitely separated from Consuelo. Her father returns to Paris on Monday. I have suggested to her that you would be very willing to go and stay with her for a while, as I cannot bear to think of her being all alone during these dark days.

Winston was desperately keen to be fair to both parties. He tried to persuade Sunny to agree to a legal separation where the custody of the children would be shared jointly and no accusations of infidelity by either side would be pressed. He was also at Sunny's right hand when it came to legal matters, writing to Consuelo's lawyer, Sir George Lewis, on 29 October 1906:

> The Duke of Marlborough has sent me a wire he received from you today requesting him to meet you without fail at 1pm tomorrow and he has

asked me to communicate with you to know if you would like me to be present also. I am at your assistance if you want me and please send me a wire on receipt of this to the G.W.R. [Great Western Railway] Boardroom at Paddington Station.

The meeting was no doubt to try and conclude the legal separation. With Winston's assistance, an agreement looked likely by Christmas 1906 but then Sunny's imperious, vindictive pride intervened. Consuelo's bellicose mother, Alva, known to her son-in-law as 'the old hag', mindful of her daughter's reputation, insisted on a clause preventing Sunny from making allegations in public about Consuelo and allowing her to visit Blenheim to keep up appearances. This was too much for Sunny who refused to sign the legal separation. Winston was furious. As his anger boiled over Sunny accused his cousin of colluding with Alva. It was the closest the two cousins came to a serious split in their lives. On 7 January an exasperated Winston wrote an indignant letter to his cousin which he wisely decided not to send fearing Sunny's wrath:

> As I fully expected, everything is back on a war basis....of course I cannot save you from yourself. If you cannot fight and will not make peace you must just be hunted down and butchered. When I think how near we were to a satisfactory settlement it makes me heartsick to see you cast away your last chance of a decent life by folly and weakness....All you were asked to do is give up the pleasure of blackguarding your wife. Rather than surrender that, you will immerse yourself in such shame and public hatred that no one will ever be able to help you any more....Why on earth can't you face the situation like a man? Do your best to help Consuelo to have a fair chance in life under the new conditions and forget for a moment your petty pride, your shoddy consistency.

It was Sunny's pride that stood in the way of a settlement. He was convinced that Consuelo was to blame as she had erred before him. While this was true, at the time of the separation, Sunny was having an affair with Gladys Deacon whom he would marry some fifteen years later. Sunny's champions, Winston, Ivor Guest and Hugh Cecil, intimate as such in their correspondence and the American press were making similar accusations in their reports on the separation. It appears that

Sunny's father-in-law, William K. Vanderbilt was also abreast of events, writing to him on 11 October 1906:

> You dwell upon the impropriety of my daughter's conduct but do not mention the fact that you have never been faithful to her either in mind or body since the beginning of your married life (I mention no names but am aware of the facts).

Thankfully, early in the New Year a settlement was agreed by the warring parties but not before Winston had received a sharp letter from the Blenheim land agent, Mr Angas, asking him to remove his polo ponies from the Estate. Following the settlement, Sunny wrote a letter of reconciliation to Winston, thanking him for his assistance in the matter and Consuelo headed off to her father's yacht in the Mediterranean. There were further ruptures in the two cousins' relationship over the years to come but nothing that seriously endangered the lasting friendship engendered by such close family ties. Sunny was left a broken man and for a while he refused to speak to close friends leaving him isolated, bitter and depressed. Jennie wrote to Winston on 13 December 1907:

> I saw Sunny at Evelyn Ker's wedding – I thought he looked thin and seedy. Where poor Sunny spends Xmas I don't know. I am told he is trying to let Blenheim. Might as well let a white elephant.

Aside from an intense pride in their own family heritage and a fascination for politics these two ambitious young Churchills had much else in common; a keen sense of history, skilled horsemanship, soldiering with the yeomanry and a love of overseas travel. On 11 September 1905 Winston wrote to Lord Rosebery:

> I am going abroad for a fortnight at the end of this month to inspect chateaux on the Loire with Sunny. After that, Blenheim.

Again, in late summer 1907, Sunny, no doubt trying to escape the sour atmosphere in London surrounding his separation from Consuelo, met Winston and F.E. Smith in Venice. The latter drove south in a car lent by Freddie Guest, who at the last moment failed to join the party and consequently was replaced by Colonel Gordon Wilson, Sunny's uncle. The group moved on to Moravia to shoot partridge and hares, finally ending up in Malta staying in the Old Palace of the Grand Masters of the Knights of Malta. Winston wrote to Pamela Lytton from Venice:

> Sunny is glad to get me here. All his old friends are in the canals but he does not dare to go and see any of them except for a minute or two because of gossip. He is alone and quite embittered. But he has only to keep his head high and to hold on for two or three years for all to come right for him. Today I am going at 10.30am to row about in a gondola with Gladys.

It was on these frequent overseas visits that Sunny spent time with his mistress, Gladys Deacon.

Sunny's first class eye and exquisite sense of taste were honed on these frequent pilgrimages to the Continent, Winston writing in his cousin's obituary:

> Sunny was a very considerable connoisseur, not so much of pictures but of works of art and furniture. He cultivated this taste by visiting all the galleries and inspecting all the treasures of Europe. He acquired a very considerable amateur knowledge in this absorbing sphere.

On 28 July 1900 Winston's mother, Jennie, married the twenty-six year old George Cornwallis-West and it was Sunny that gave the bride away with a 'solid phalanx' of Churchills evident amongst the guests. It meant a great deal to Winston to have the Duke's unwavering and very public support for his mother's marriage. The union was not without controversy as George was considerably younger than Jennie. Winston would have to wait another eight years before securing his partner, the much more suitable Clementine Hozier. He evidently managed to tolerate Sunny's arrogant high Conservatism but it was not the same with Clemmie who constantly encouraged her husband's radicalism. She rarely felt comfortable in the company of Winston's Conservative friends such as Sunny and the hard-drinking F.E. Smith. Much to her consternation both men were present when Winston first took Clemmie to Blenheim in August 1908 which would, in the event, end happily in a marriage proposal.

Winston and Clementine, the newlyweds on British Army manoeuvres.
Winston is in the uniform of the QOOH.

If Clemmie never really warmed to Sunny at least she witnessed some
of his better qualities on that momentous initial visit to the Palace. In
persuading her to join him at Blenheim Winston wrote:

> I hope you will like my friend and fascinate him with those strange mys-
> terious eyes of yours, whose secret I have been trying so hard to learn…
> He is quite different from me, understanding women thoroughly, getting
> in touch with them at once….whereas I am stupid and clumsy in that
> relation and naturally quite self-reliant and self-contained.

This was a very candid comment by Winston as Sunny, unlike his cousin,
possessed a more ardent sex drive and enjoyed female company. On their
second morning at Blenheim Winston made an assignation with Clemmie to walk in the gardens following breakfast. Having little sense of
punctuality, he failed to make the breakfast table. Sunny, having been

forewarned of Winston's marital plans, immediately noticed Clemmie's distress, and in exercising his considerable charm and good manners, took her for a drive in the Park. Sunny's kindness was in evidence again the following month when he placed Blenheim at Winston's disposal for the wedding night.

On 18 August Winston wrote to Sunny asking him to become his trustee and his best man. Sunny readily accepted the first request but surprisingly declined the latter replying:

> I regard all marriages as solemn events and in the case of a dear friend and relation the occasion is a trying one. I hope you will allow me to spare myself the mingled pleasure and pain of such a ceremony. Believe me my thoughts will be with you though I myself will be absent.

Maybe his own memories in this direction were too embarrassing and painful but perhaps it was more likely that he had his own prior commitments on the Continent with Gladys Deacon. In the event, Hugh Cecil took over the role of best man. Sunny did however, continue with great gentility and, it would seem, with a touch of irony:

> Your engagement has given me much pleasure and a great deal of satisfaction. It is a joy to feel that you are so happy and that you realise in ensuring the contentment of another being, lies in no small way the solace and also the enjoyment of life.

Being sensitive to these close family ties, Clemmie managed to treat Sunny with a polite reserve, until another visit to Blenheim in the autumn of 1913 ended in a fracas which would result in a distinct chill between the cousins for over a year.

Although Sunny and Winston did not always take kindly to their respective others it was nothing compared to their political differences after Winston left the Conservative Party and joined the Liberal Party in 1904. Matters reached a head between the ducal and radical branches of the family over the 'People's Budget' of 1909 and the ensuing General Election needed to push the money bill through the House of Lords.

In order to pay for Dreadnought battleships and the Liberals' programme of social reform, Lloyd George had for the first time

*A cartoon of Winston consoling his cousin Sunny over the introduction
of Lloyd George's 'People's Budget' in 1909.*

differentiated in his first budget between the rates of tax on earned and
unearned income, raised death duties and introduced a land tax. Herbert
Henry Asquith, the Prime Minister, correctly predicted that it would be
the latter which would 'set the heather alight'. And how right he was.
Sunny was furious about the new taxes as was his cousin, Ivor Guest,

who went so far as to threaten resignation as a Member of Parliament.

David Lloyd George, the Chancellor of the Exchequer, who interestingly Winston had been allowed to bring to Blenheim in July 1908, used his 'People's Budget' and its opposition in the House of Lords as a means to stir up class warfare. On 30 July 1909 he pilloried the Dukes in his notorious Limehouse speech stating: 'A fully equipped Duke costs as much to keep up as two Dreadnoughts' and again some months later: 'The aristocracy is like cheese, the older it is, the higher it becomes.'

Encouraged by the efforts of his bellicose cabinet colleague, Winston himself went on the offensive, rather foolishly attacking his own class. At Leicester on 4 September he referred to the Dukes as 'ornamental creatures' who had no business meddling in politics and ought to be content 'to lead quiet delicate sheltered lives', and 'do not let us be too hard on them, it is almost like teasing goldfish.' To his credit Sunny did not rise to this cousinly provocation, Violet Bonham Carter writing in her biography of Winston noted:

> Winston replied loyally that though Sunny did not like the Budget he had kept out of the scrum. He had kept his hair on and his scales on.

Roy Jenkins agreed that Sunny demonstrated both composure and stoicism, writing in his biography of Churchill:

> As Dukes went, Marlborough remained relatively restrained unlike the Duke of Beaufort who said he would like to see Winston Churchill and Lloyd George in the midst of twenty couples of dog hounds.

Winston had a serious conflict of interest. Lloyd George was an important political ally yet Winston also had many rich friends and relations. Confident of his ability to manage both factions and no doubt with Sunny and F.E. Smith in mind, he wrote to the King on 9 August 1911:

> Extremely good personal relations are maintained by persons most strongly opposed to one another.

It is remarkable that the close friendship of the Churchill cousins survived the political theatre of the Asquith administration from the 'People's

Budget' of 1909 until the Parliament Bill of 1911. The latter depriving the Lords of their power of veto and most dramatically of all, as far as Sunny was concerned, ending hundreds of years of rule by the aristocracy in Britain. It was all a far cry from the renowned Blenheim rally of August 1901 for the Conservative and Liberal Unionist Party. This gathering, attended by 120 Members of Parliament together with over 3,000 supporters, was hosted by Sunny who shared the platform harmoniously with Winston.

Family ties

Whatever personal differences Sunny and Winston exhibited during these years, in Winston's eyes the family bond was always paramount. Ever since his separation from Consuelo, Sunny's name had been deliberately omitted from the list of those invited to lunch with King George after the Garter ceremony, as the new monarch adhered rigidly to the convention that no divorced or even separated husband or wife could be received at court. On 21 May 1911, Winston wrote to the King, on behalf of Sunny, pleading that a limited dispensation could be obtained and no further snub be inflicted on the Duke:

> The Duke has been unhappy in his married life but he is respected in his county and his home. He has three times been chosen as Mayor of Woodstock. He commands a regiment of Your Majesty's Yeomanry. He is a member of the Privy Council. He has served in the field. He has been Under-Secretary of State for the Colonies and it is not at all improbable that he would receive office, subject to Your Majesty's approval if a Conservative Government was returned to power.

The King graciously conceded to his request after a lengthy debate with his private secretary, Lord Knollys.

In October 1911 as Anglo-German relations deteriorated Winston was moved to the Admiralty. In the spring of 1912 the First Lord still found the time to ask his cousin down to Portland to visit the fleet and watch target practice from the Admiralty yacht, the Neptune. Sunny had to leave early to have his left shoulder 'electrified'. Correspondence between the cousins later that year points not only to Sunny's poor health but also to a wicked sense of humour. From France, where Sunny was staying with Gladys, he wrote:

Sunny was most disapproving of Winston's passion for flying, considering it far too dangerous for a family man.

I am recuperating in Paris and can now walk out for a couple of hours every day. The weather being beautiful helps me to make a good recovery. F.E. has kept me well informed of events at Westminster. I purchased you today a Xmas present which is somewhat premature. I have been shocked at the manner in which you display your person when travelling to and from the bathroom and I am making an effort to find you an appropriate leaf.

The following year Winston took up flying. On 12 March Sunny, with his cousin's best interests at heart, wrote:

I do not suppose I shall get the chance of writing you many more letters if you continue your journeys in the air. Really, I consider that you owe it to your wife and family and friends to desist from a practice or pastime – whichever you call it – which is fraught with so much danger to life. It is really wrong of you....

While Sunny cared deeply about Winston's wellbeing their politics remained fractious. Lloyd George was still at his aggressive best on 22 October 1913 giving an address at Swindon on Land Reform. The following day Clemmie and her sister, Nellie, were reading the speech in the Long Library at Blenheim and showing animated signs of approval, which, needless to say, upset their host. That same morning she wrote to Winston:

> Sunny is *au fond* broad-minded about the land taxes but he does not let it appear on the surface and indulges in the sourness and bitterness of a crab apple! But he works it all off at tennis.

Later in the day when Sunny noticed Clemmie communicating with Lloyd George over certain political arrangements which she and Winston were involved with, he finally lost his temper, growling: 'Please Clemmie, would you not mind writing to that horrible little man on Blenheim writing paper.' This was all too much for Clemmie who packed her bags and headed for Woodstock railway station. The Churchills would not be spending the coming Christmas at Blenheim.

The rift was finally healed when war broke out in 1914. In September Sunny and his two sons, Bert and Ivor, visited Winston at the Admiralty. As the new First Lord, he was busily engaged in hunting down the German cruiser, the Goeben. Sunny asked Winston if he could help find him a position to help with the war effort. As a Conservative he was barred from having a political appointment and not being a professional soldier he was too old to serve at the Front. Winston duly approached Kitchener, the Secretary of State for War, who agreed to attach Sunny to the War Office as a Special Messenger carrying despatches to Sir John French in France. On 13 September 1914 Winston wrote to Kitchener:

> I am touched by the promptness with which you have looked after Marlborough. It is a great pleasure to work with you and the two departments work well together.

In May 1915 owing to the disastrous Gallipoli landings in the Dardanelles Winston was forced from the Admiralty. Writing to his cousin on 24 May Sunny remarked:

Pro tem Lloyd George has done you in. I am deeply grieved for you that you have lost control of those affairs which so engrossed your energies. I think that you have been unfairly treated; in politics we live above or below our form, seldom on a just level.

He was offered a minor consolation post in the cabinet by Asquith as Chancellor of the Duchy of Lancaster. Sunny wrote sympathetically to Winston:

The fare is poor but I suppose you will think it wisest to live on emergency rations pro tem. I think that the Admiralty has lost all initiative and push since your departure and a complete static selfish atmosphere seems to prevail in that Department. An atmosphere congenial to A.J.B.'s [Arthur James Balfour's] temperament. It is a pity you are not there to give the officials some inspiration.

Everyone was contemplating the path of Winston's future political career, Asquith writing to his lover, Venetia Stanley earlier in the year:

It is not easy to see what Winston's career is going to be. He is to some extent blanketed by E. Grey [Foreign Secretary] and Lloyd George and has no personal following. He is always hankering after coalitions and re-groupings mainly designed (as one thinks) to bring in F.E. Smith and perhaps the Duke of Marlborough. I think his future is one of the most puzzling enigmas in politics, don't you?

So even the Prime Minister had wind of the bond between the two cousins!

It is notable that during the summer of 1915 while under such political pressure Winston found the time to ride to his cousin's rescue. On the death of Lord Jersey, the much-coveted post of Lord Lieutenant of Oxfordshire became vacant and Sunny with his medieval sense of self-importance felt he was the rightful successor. Ever since his supposed scandalous separation from Consuelo, Sunny had lived the life of a morose recluse at Blenheim and was shunned by many of the local landed gentry. Making enemies of influential neighbours did not help his cause and he was in danger of being passed over for the Lieutenancy. That the county set felt their local duke was a member of 'the fast set' and perhaps even a little 'nouveau', is evidenced by Consuelo in *The Glitter and the Gold*:

> There is always a certain jealousy of what is considered the most important family or the finest estate in the county. It was apparent that the older families whose roots were imbedded in Oxfordshire regarded the Churchills, who moved there in the eighteenth century, rather as the Pilgrim Fathers looked upon later arrivals in America. Perhaps also to impress me they stressed their ancient lineage, seeming to imply that lives lived in a long-ago past conferred a greater dignity on those who lived in the present.

A paranoid Sunny felt that Consuelo was marshalling his enemies such as Lord Saye and Sele, an Oxfordshire county councillor known by Gladys as 'Lord Stay and Steal', to exert pressure on Prime Minister Asquith to appoint an alternative candidate. All turned out well in the end, as John Pearson in *Citadel of the Heart* observed:

> Churchill, obsessed as always with his close relations, solemnly agreed that this would be unthinkable – 'a terrible reproach to the family'. He used all his powers of persuasion with the Lord Chamberlain and ensured that Sunny was appointed.

On 16 July 1915 Winston wrote to his uncle, Lord Lansdowne:

> On general grounds it may be said in times like these Lord Lieutenancies should be held if possible by persons of military experience and Sunny with twenty two years' service, including a full period in command and war service with the yeomanry, has very decided qualifications of this character. It has occurred to me that this fact might be held in the present circumstances to outweigh altogether the social inconvenience of his separation from his wife, especially as that occurred so long ago that it is now generally accepted as a matter of the past.

In the autumn of 1915 Winston took the decision to leave the government altogether. In November he delivered his resignation speech to the House of Commons before leaving for active service in the trenches. His

The Prime Minister, Lloyd George and Winston Churchill, the two men responsible for bringing Sunny back into Government in 1917.

oration centred on defending his role in the Gallipoli campaign. Sunny wrote on the eve of his departure:

> It was an excellent exposition of your case and I rejoice. I wish though you had left out the part criticising Fisher. You raise a controversy which his friends will take up as a challenge. In case I don't see you before you go – may Providence protect you and may we see you 'ere long.

On 15 December, having turned his back on politics, Winston wrote Sunny a quite remarkable letter about life at the Front with the Grenadier Guards:

> My feeling that my greatest work is still to do is strong in me and the experience of adversity which I am now going through will, if I survive, give to my character qualities which otherwise might never have been developed.

These words, which he could probably only write to Sunny, would prove truly prophetic. Winston never doubted his own abilities and had exceptional vision. In the New Year Winston, now commanding the 6th Royal Scots Fusileers, gave his cousin his views on soldiering:

> If I am killed at the head of my battalion it will be an honourable and dignified finale. Do you think I should deserve the family motto, 'Faithful yet Unfortunate'? I am now passing through a stage in my journey quite beyond any that my father had to traverse. Your letter and affection are a great pleasure to me. We must always try and keep together as the world grows grey.

Sunny returned the compliment in May 1916 asking Winston and Diana down to Blenheim saying he had not seen his goddaughter for years. Sunny congratulated Winston, recently returned from the Front, on his latest speech in the Commons. He then proceeded to castigate the whole War Office administration suggesting that Winston should replace Kitchener and Haig should take over from Robertson as Chief of Staff.

Sunny even found time to visit Winston at the Front, presumably when performing his duties as a King's Messenger. Later in the war when Winston was back in government he sought out Sunny's eldest son, the Marquess of Blandford who was serving at the Front with the Life Guards. He wrote to Sunny:

> During my visit to the trenches in France last week I made a pilgrimage to a remote village called Jeancourt very near the front line for the purpose of seeking out Blandford if I could. I found him prowling about halfway up a long valley looking at guns and horses and things…. He looked very well and quite happy and was, I think, agreeably surprised by the advent of an avuncular relation.

Nowhere was the political divide between Sunny and Winston more evident than in the latter stages of the war. The cousins were both serving in Lloyd George's Coalition, when in late 1917 Winston, as Minister for Munitions, faced a strike by armament workers on the Clyde. Winston according to Boris Johnson, sorted it out by getting them in for tea and cake and bunging them 12%. In order to allay some of the workers' grievances Winston promised: 'No worker should be penalised for belonging to a trade union or taking part in a trade dispute.'[4] This was too much for Sunny who had a weather eye on his escalating wage bill at Blenheim, writing to Gladys Deacon on 5 February 1918:

> I do not mean to go into their house again – till order reigns in this country – and they have learnt their proper place. That 12.5% I can never forgive. It means 150 million a year more in wages. I wonder what the French would have done to their Minister of Munitions.

The altercation did not last. Sunny and Ivor dined with Winston in Paris the following year and in the ensuing months they kept in touch through written correspondence, either covering the domestic political situation or the Paris Peace Conference. On 12 April 1919, Winston wrote with his usual foresight:

> We cannot afford to go on maltreating the Germans while we have the Bolshevik peril on our hands.

Cordial relations between the cousins continued during 1919 especially after a horrific influenza epidemic swept the country. More people died than in the whole course of the war. Clemmie and a number of her domestic servants succumbed to the illness and Sunny offered Winston his London house as a place of convalescence. Winston wrote:

> My dear Sunny, many thanks for your letter. I have been using the house all this week and it has been a great convenience to me. Clemmie is now much better. I propose to let her sleep here Monday and Tuesday night, as Dean Trench Street requires to be properly disinfected after all the illness we have had there.

In June 1921, once his divorce from Consuelo had finally been granted, Sunny married Gladys. He wrote to Winston:

> I was much gratified to get your letter and to receive the goodwill of Clemmie and you on the occasion of my engagement. I think that Gladys and I will be happy in our lives together. She is a very remarkable woman and

Winston Churchill in the Long Library whilst staying at Blenheim in the 1920s. Note the new bookcases Sunny incorporated into the refurbishment of the library. The Sunderland Library having been sold by his grandfather, the 7th Duke of Marlborough, in 1882.

possesses the power of attracting all classes of individuals among the population of Paris to herself. A task by no means easy, politicians, artists, 'May Fairies', all stream along to see her. The round of social entertainment will soon become intolerable. We are going to be married at the British Consulate if Lord Curzon will give the Consul General leave to celebrate the marriage. This he has the power to do. The French press have paid tribute to Gladys' personality and all sorts of individuals write to me offering their congratulations. I shall hope to see you before too long.

Lord Saye and Sele would return to haunt Sunny. In October 1922 his lordship visited the offices of Sunny's solicitor, Sir George Lewis, to ask him to try and persuade the Duke to give up the Lieutenancy following his recent divorce from Consuelo, despite being separated for over fifteen years. Sir George wrote a memo to his client on the subject dated 17 October:

I asked Lord Saye and Sele why on earth he interfered in this matter; was it a private or a public feeling that prompted him to do so? He said, entirely public. He also said he had no feeling against the Duke of Marlborough before his divorce case, he frequently saw him and had personal relations with him. I said that it seemed strange that he should take upon himself to write in the way he did and it did not appear that anyone had asked him to do so. He said he did it for the County and that his family had lived in the County for 600 years and that he represented one of the most prominent families there and that when the Queen recently came to Oxford she would not see the Duke of Marlborough.

Needless to say Sunny held his ground in the face of this provincial onslaught.

An interesting example of Sunny's old-world conservatism that particularly irked Winston raised its head when the Churchills purchased Chartwell Manor in September 1922. Chartwell was a manor house of Elizabethan origins with splendid views over the Weald. The house which was purchased for £5,000 in a dilapidated condition necessitated considerable further expenditure. Winston therefore requested that a mortgage be raised by the two trustees, his brother Jack and Sunny. Winston wanted to spend an initial £7,000 on the refurbishment of the property financed by way of a £3,500 mortgage and the balance through share sales. Jack, who was a stockbroker in the City, was in total agreement but much to Winston's ire, Sunny dug in his heels. The Duke felt that the purpose of a share portfolio was to augment the family income and the current deflationary environment was not the right time to borrow against property. He also insisted that the trustees should not borrow more than 50% against the value of the property. Winston wrote a testy letter back to his cousin:

> You would I think take a great responsibility if in the exercise of what is a personal view you prevented the mortgage being effected and subsequently it was found that the shares had lost the rise that they had achieved and that the value of the property on which the mortgage could be secured had been greatly advanced.

In the 1920's the two cousins would see less of each other as Winston reignited his remarkable political career and the new country house in

Kent made increasing demands on his time. In addition, there was little love lost between Winston and Sunny's new wife, Gladys Deacon. After a day in Venice with Gladys, Winston dismissed her in a letter to Pamela Lytton as 'one of those strange glittering beings with whom I have little or nothing in common.' For her part, Hugo Vickers relates in his biography *Gladys* how much she disliked Winston: 'He was incapable of love.' She believed that: 'He was in love with his own image – his reflection in the mirror.' At Blenheim he always had to be in the centre of everything that happened: 'I watched him all the time, he took an instant dislike to me... I knew him from top to bottom... He was entirely out for Winston.' She was equally dismissive about his wife, Clementine. Vickers continues: 'Gladys said: 'You could not discuss a thing with her. She had no opinions, only convictions.'

Enduring friendship

The two cousins still kept in touch and Sunny was always interested in Winston's political career. In the autumn of 1922 Winston lost his Dundee seat at the General Election. He wrote to Sunny from the south of France:

> It has been pleasant out here and such a relief after all these years not to have a score of big anxieties and puzzles on one's shoulders. The Government moulders away but I must confess myself more interested in the past than present.

Winston enclosed a copy of his new book, *The World Crisis* while at the same time he was being encouraged by the literary world to write a magnum opus on his ancestor, John, 1st Duke of Marlborough. As Winston was considering moving back into the Conservative fold, Sunny replied with typically sound advice:

> It is not easy to probe into the immediate future but I personally think you are wise to preserve a detached position from the Tory Party until you can command your terms and get hold of the title deeds.

Correspondence over the last years of Sunny's life centred largely on either the Indian Empire Society or Winston's developing biography of Duke John. Not surprisingly for two ex-Colonial Office ministers, Sunny

*Sunny and Clementine
staying with Bendor
Westminster for the Grand
National, circa 1930.*

and Winston were passionate Imperialists and desperate to keep India in the Empire. The independence movement led by Gandhi was gathering pace and a power struggle was building between Moslems and Hindus. In early 1931 one thousand Indians were killed at Cawnpore in communal violence. Winston was keen that Sunny should become more involved in the Indian Empire Society and specifically chair a proposed rally at the Albert Hall. The Society was comprised of people who were concerned about events in India and whose views differed from those of the Socialist Government or the Viceroy. The aim was to give public expression to their point of view. Winston also wanted Sunny to speak on a forthcoming vote in the Lords, 'where opinion is moving in our direction'. On 25 April he wrote to Sunny:

> I think you should endeavour to speak very briefly in this debate, ten minutes would be quite enough, on the principle of welcoming the firmer declaration which will have been made and also drawing attention to the horrible affair at Cawnpore.

Sunny on the steps above his beloved terraces. From left to right:- Gwendoline and her husband Jack Spencer-Churchill (Winston's brother), Sunny and Lady Sarah Wilson, Sunny's indomitable aunt, circa 1928.

Probably on account of his deteriorating health together with commitments at Blenheim Sunny declined to participate.

Sunny played an important role in facilitating the production of Winston's epic biography on the 1st Duke of Marlborough. Winston stayed at Blenheim the weekend of 17 January 1931 when Sunny invited the publisher to lunch, 'to discuss the possibilities of a luxury edition'. The previous week Winston wrote to his cousin asking him if he would entertain the Professor of Modern History at Oxford 'to stay and dine' as he was a 'great champion of Duke John' and he would very much like to see Blenheim and the tapestries. Again, in March 1933, he asked whether a photographer could be sent down to Blenheim and would Sunny kindly propose some suitable family portraits to include in the biography?

In September 1932 Winston visited all Marlborough's major battlefields. He kept Sunny in touch with his excursions giving him a taste of the glorious prose that would grace the coming book. On 25 September he wrote to Sunny of Marlborough's departure from Coblenz to Blenheim in the summer of 1704 by way of the Danube valley:

The enemy still thought it was a campaign in Alsace; but no, a fortnight later the long scarlet columns swung off to the Danube and the great strategic design which altered the history of Europe became apparent. This marvellous march was distinguished for its absolute secrecy and mystery – no one knew, not the Queen, not Sarah, not the English Government, except Eugene; and secondly for the extraordinary elaboration with which every detail was worked out. New boots for the troops were found in Coblenz; food and wine appeared at every camping ground as if by magic; all the soldiers had to do was to pitch the tents and boil their kettles.

And of the campaigns in the Low Countries he wrote:

One day I am going to ask you to give me some money, £2-300, and I will give half as much as I ask you to give in order to put up a few granite stones with bronze tablets at Ramilles, Oudenarde and Malplaquet. The governments of these countries would be very willing. It is a shame that these historical fields should have no record upon them. The French have put up a monument at Malplaquet to Villars and Boufflers but nothing marks the British victory.

Sunny himself was occupied with executing his improvements at Blenheim and his masterpiece was nearing completion. He was proud of his project having mentioned to Winston during the remodelling of the terraces on 12 July 1928:

I hope you will come and see me here before you retire to the country. I want you to see the work on the terraces.

The two cousins still relished each other's company. The mutual support of earlier years remained as strong as ever, Sunny offering to hold the reception for Diana Churchill's wedding at his London residence at Carlton House Terrace in December 1932. Whenever he was needed, Winston was at his cousin's side, whether at Sunny's 60th birthday party at Blenheim or, finally, at his deathbed in June 1934. On 21 July Sir Archibald Sinclair wrote to Winston:

I think much of you in your sorrows at losing so suddenly a friend and kinsman who was so dear to you. You are surrounded by devoted friends but none, I know, can replace the two whom you have so recently lost.[5]

According to Charles Moran, Winston's personal physician, Churchill was asked after the war which year of his life he would most like to relive. He replied 1940 and added:

> I wish certain people could have been alive to see the events of the last years of the war, my father and mother, F.E., Arthur Balfour and Sunny.

This statement says it all. Sunny might not have been a political heavy-weight like Smith or Balfour but he was head of the Churchill family, hereditary tenant of Winston's spiritual home, Blenheim Palace, Winston's closest first cousin and as such the greatest Englishman's best life-long friend.

8

Gladys

Shortly after 1900, Gladys Deacon, a remarkable young American of both beauty and intelligence, began to realise a childhood dream. Having met Sunny on a summer visit to London, this ambitious teenage woman from a privileged East Coast background, would in a short time become his lover. Some twenty years later this relationship would lead to marriage, her elevation to mistress of Blenheim Palace and her eventual destruction.

This was an era when the society press on both sides of the Atlantic was full of gossip about the 'dollar princesses', who as 'colonial heiresses', were being spirited away to Britain in droves to replenish the finances of many a decaying stately home. Although by comparison of more modest means, Gladys was determined not to be outdone by her wealthier compatriots, particularly one, Consuelo Vanderbilt. In October 1895 when she was fourteen years old, Gladys wrote to her mother, Florence Baldwin:

> I suppose you have read about the engagement of the Duke of Marlborough. Oh dear me, if I was only a little older I might catch him yet! But Helas! I am too young though mature in the arts of women's witchcraft and what is the use of one without the other? And I will have to give up all chance to get Marlborough.

Sunny Marlborough may not have enjoyed the material wealth of other British aristocrats but he was a Duke and even better, a Duke with his

Gladys as a child.

own Palace. Consequently he was regarded by the American press as the most eligible bachelor ever to arrive on the East Coast of America. In 1900 he left home for South Africa to both serve his country in the Boer War and escape his failing marriage to America's richest heiress, Consuelo Vanderbilt. Having carried out her duty and produced an heir in 1897 this 'pressed' bride, perhaps understandably, freely embarked on a number of high profile affairs thus demonstrating her New World sense of liberal pride and independence.

On his return from the South African War, Sunny met Gladys at a society event in London and both he and Consuelo fell under the spell of her charm. Consuelo wrote in *The Glitter and the Gold*:

> Gladys Deacon was a beautiful girl endowed with a brilliant intellect. Possessed of exceptional powers of conversation, she could enlarge on

any subject in an interesting and amusing manner. I was soon subjected by the charm of her companionship and we began a friendship which only ended years later.

It is obvious that Consuelo was as much taken by Gladys as her husband and dare one might conjecture that she encouraged Sunny in his amorous adventures in this direction?

It appears that the teenage Gladys was blessed with many and various gifts. According to Gladys' biographer, Hugo Vickers, her stunning beauty was characterised by 'a good Hellenic profile and enormous, staring, bright blue eyes.' In 1896 she left America with her mother for the European Continent and completed her education in Paris, Bonn and Florence. Gladys was an exceptional student. As early as fourteen she could sing and play the mandolin. She had begun to learn German and taken an interest in the theatre and opera. In addition she began to build up a library of rare books. By the age of eighteen she had studied mathematics and Latin, emerging with seven languages. She had also acquired a wide general knowledge, a fascination for mythology and a lifelong love of art, literature and poetry. Vickers relates how:

> Her powers of conversation, her extraordinary use of the written word and her intriguing personality had an astonishing effect on nearly everyone she met in her long life.

It is hardly surprising that while living in Paris, Gladys was swept up in a world of aesthetes, academics and artists. The man most responsible for launching her into this Bohemian world was Comte Robert de Montesquiou, an eccentric and flamboyant patron of the arts, poet and author. It was he who introduced her to fashionable society painters such as Boldini, Helleu and Jacques-Emile Blanche; all three demonstrated an enthusiastic appreciation of her youthful beauty. Her real mentor and confident was Bernard Berenson, the celebrated art critic. Having first met in St Moritz in 1899, Gladys became close friends of the Berensons and a regular visitor to their villa, I Tatti, in the hills above Florence. When the Berensons were going through a difficult period in their marriage in 1901, Bernard wrote to Mary, his wife, telling her that he loved Gladys very much and would have liked to have married her.

Male and female alike quickly became intoxicated by Gladys's unique personality, her powers of conversation, intelligence and humour. Mary Berenson saw two sides of this 'brilliant, beautiful, cruel, selfish, untrained individual', writing in her diary for February 1902:

> Gladys has been enchanting but tiring. A wonderful creature, but too young to talk to as an equal and so much of a born actress to take quite seriously. But so beautiful, so graceful, so changeful in a hundred moods, so brilliant that it is enough to turn anybody's head.

A further entry reads:

> Gladys is of course interested in nothing except herself or what touched her and being so brilliant a creature she cannot be put down as so young a girl naturally would be.

It is difficult to speculate as to when Sunny's affair with Gladys began yet he wrote his first passionate love letter to her from Harrogate in August 1901 sending her 'his fond remembrances' and insinuating that it was his hope that the relationship would progress to a more intimate level. He was clearly smitten. At much the same time she was enjoying a close friendship with Consuelo, the latter writing to her from Blenheim:

> Whenever I am depressed I imagine myself in Italy with you – not with the Italians – just reading, contemplating everything beautiful and breathing in the spirit of the universe in great deep breaths – uplifting and refreshing.

It is probable that Gladys was holding off Sunny at this time for strategic purposes which would have been frustrating as he knew all too well that Consuelo had been unfaithful to him for the best part of three years. In order to win over her Duke Gladys would almost certainly have 'played hard to get' at this stage in their relationship. Meanwhile, well-publicised flirtations with the Crown Prince of Prussia together with aristocrats such as the Guest brothers and the heir to the Duke of Newcastle must surely have kept Sunny on his mettle?

Bearing in mind their respective lifestyles it is hard to see how Sunny and Gladys managed to find the time to spend together let alone to develop

Gladys demonstrating both the classic Grecian profile and her love of Blenheim spaniels.

a more intimate relationship. She, with her fluent French, felt much more at home in France than she ever did in London. Sunny had his commitments at Blenheim and in 1903 Balfour, the Prime Minister, promoted him to the time-consuming office of Under-Secretary of State for the Colonies. Gladys took the London season by storm in both the Coronation Year and 1903, retiring to Blenheim at various points over the summer months to restore her health and energy. Sunny for his part would make visits to Paris when his busy schedule allowed, as noted by Vickers:

> The Duke, recently returned from the Delhi Durbar, arrived in Paris for a few days. Mrs Baldwin was suspicious that Gladys was up to something with him and worried that she might elope with him just to spite Consuelo.

The Berensons were particularly concerned for their rudderless, muddled friend, complete with her 'excited brain'. They just wanted her to fall into the right hands.

The security that the Berensons craved for Gladys was even less likely to materialise in 1904 when Mrs Baldwin and her daughters moved to Rome. She was soon courted by a series of aristocratic suitors including the Duke of Camastra and Prince Torlonia. Perhaps her favourite and the man some say she should have married was Roffredo Caetani, second son of the Duke of Sermoneta. He was an attractive and cultured bachelor of thirty-two in addition to being a gifted composer. Yet none of her Italian liaisons developed into anything too serious. Did she have a preference for an English aristocrat? She toyed with the broken-hearted Lord Brooke and spread the word that she was all but engaged to the Earl of Warwick's heir. She almost certainly frightened off many of her potential suitors.

There were two distinct sides to Gladys's personality. One, the bewitchingly beautiful woman with wonderful powers of intellect and conversation who people found both fascinating and irresistible. The other, a restless, insolent, cruel and self-absorbed individual who projected herself as unpredictable, intimidating and untrustworthy. A friend of the Berensons, Mabel Dodge, wrote that 'she loved only herself and she was not bothered about lovers.' Perhaps she was still living her childhood fantasy, saving herself for her English Duke and at the same time securing herself the perverse satisfaction of upstaging America's foremost heiress?

In October 1906 Gladys came a step closer to realising her dream when the Marlboroughs were granted a legal separation, although any question of divorce at this time was next to impossible in such elevated social circles. Life reverted to its frustrating normality for Sunny. Gladys was back on the Continent spending most of her time in Paris making new conquests with her usual regularity, whereas he could not be seen publicly with his mistress in London. Among her new conquests the author, Marcel Proust, said of her: 'I never saw a girl with such beauty, such magnificent intelligence, such goodness and charm.' In the summer of 1908, while staying in Innsbruck, she met the philosopher, Hermann Keyserling who referred to her as 'this woman of genius.' It was love at first sight and he asked her to marry him. Keyserling, like so many before him, was ultimately rejected.

Towards the end of the year Gladys escaped both Keyserling's and her mother's clutches and went to live in Paris on her own. This new-found freedom gave Sunny the opportunity to visit her in more relaxed

Sunny on holiday with Gladys. He adored these excursions to the continent which produced such a refreshing contrast to his regulated and conservative routine at Blenheim.

circumstances. He adored these excursions to the Continent which provided such a refreshing contrast to his regulated and conservative routine at Blenheim. Their love affair took another positive step forward in 1911 when she moved to London, taking rooms in Savile Row. Consuelo was still refusing to grant Sunny a divorce and Hugo Vickers records Gladys' sorry plight:

> And so she had to be content with the role of mistress occasionally accompanying the Duke on holiday abroad and receiving him at her little London apartment.

When they were apart, particularly when Gladys returned to Rome to visit her mother, Sunny missed her terribly, enduring long periods of solitude and depression.

Gladys spent the first half of the First World War in London, becoming a naturalised British citizen in 1915. According to her biographer, her life now revolved entirely around Sunny who was busy serving as a King's Messenger, having re-joined the Army as a Staff Officer. They dined together whenever possible although Sunny worried about the

Sunny commissioned Boldini to paint Gladys' portrait in Paris in 1916.

loneliness of her lifestyle. She never really enjoyed life in London and in 1916 returned to Paris to visit her mother, old friends such as Degas, Rodin, Monet and Anatole France and most importantly, to have her portrait painted by Boldini. Using the excuse of ill health she refused to return which infuriated Sunny and led to further bouts of his famous melancholia. To make matters worse he was finding it impossible to push

Sunny overseeing the harvest. In 1917 he returned to Government having been recalled into the Lloyd George coalition as a Junior Agriculture Minister.

ahead with his divorce from Consuelo. The war had delayed the introduction of a new divorce law which would have made desertion for more than three years as one of the grounds for divorce.

Sunny and Gladys were apart for most of 1918, she in Paris and he fully occupied in London on government matters having been recalled into Lloyd George's Coalition as a Junior Agriculture Minister. Gladys' letters at this time, which are held in the Blenheim archive, tell an interesting story. She writes to him almost every day signing off, 'Goodnight MS' (My Sunny) 'from YG' (Your Gladys). As you would expect from one so intelligent, the letters are full of news covering diverse subjects such as politics, military strategy, poetry, art and financial matters. She

A grumpy looking Duke having a picnic with his cows.

was an enthusiastic investor in her own right, writing on 5 October 1918: 'U.S. stocks going badly, Oils dropping, my personal flutter of ten days ago is steady at a six point rise.' There is more frivolous coverage of social gossip, the weather, buying jewellery and family matters. She also includes newspaper cuttings on topics that would interest Sunny such as the price of lamb, political commentary and society tittle-tattle.

Gladys constantly chides Sunny for not communicating. On 8 April 1918 she writes: 'You are becoming a sort of wraith in my memory, you never tell me a thing about Blandford, the crops, the house, your family, your friends', and again in the autumn:

It's been a week today since you left and our last evening was taken by one of your family. I have had one letter from you since and I think that

A small drawing of Gladys by Boldini which today hangs in the Duke's study.

if I don't hear from you tomorrow I had better stop writing until I do.

There are recurrent references to illness and depression, the former often relating to her and the latter to Sunny. She tells Sunny to 'control your perpetual state of catastrophic outlook' and 'don't be gloomy My Sunny, after all the worst years of your life are behind you.' For her part she is frequently ill, writing from her sickbed on 29 April:

I'm going to have my hair cut, it's so long that even when plaited I can sit on it. The doctor thinks it's taking too much vitality out of me!

Gladys repeatedly deploys a poison pen in her correspondence, vitriol being bestowed on friends and family alike. On 11 March 1918 she reminds us of her dislike for Winston and his politics:

Winston is the nucleus of bolshevism. He will try to be the Czar of the future and as I have told you over and over again he is dangerous to your interests.

Doubtless because of the pending divorce and the Duke's resulting fall from grace in society, the two lovers felt that the whole world was up in arms against them. Separation compounded their misery and a general air of pessimism prevailed towards the end of the war. Gladys moped to Sunny:

At any rate the same people hate us both and that is a great exemplifier,

The happy couple finally wed at the British Embassy in Paris in June 1921.

the enemies of one are sure to be enemies of the other and we can so warn each other.

Gladys was transmitting her misery on to others. She gradually lost more of her old friends, meeting Bernard Berenson for the last time in 1919. He wrote to a friend, Umberto Morra:

> I decided to stop seeing Gladys Deacon when I convinced myself that in human relationships she offered nothing but an offensive arbitrariness, pursuing people in a flattering and ensnaring fashion, only to be able to break off with them noisily when the fancy struck her.

She did, however, accumulate new friends particularly if they were aristocratic. Following the death of her mother, Gladys acquired a small house in the South of France where she met the recently widowed Duke of Connaught, the last surviving son of Queen Victoria. Both he and, in contrast, the bohemian poet, Bob Trevelyan, fell madly in love with her.

Gladys on her wedding day.

It is thought that she might have considered marrying the 'Irish Duke' merely to have upstaged Consuelo.

Just as Gladys was settling into a new life in Nice, Consuelo decided that after some fifteen years it was time to marry again. Having fallen in love with French aviator, Jacques Balsan, she agreed to grant Sunny a divorce. A petition was entered into on 10 November 1920 and the decree became absolute the following summer. Gladys's childhood ambition was about to be recognised. She would abandon both her beloved bohemian existence and independence for a monotonous life at Blenheim. Although elated about her engagement, she was scared for her future, writing in her diary on 2 June 1922:

> I feel again the thrill of terror which ran through me when I read it in the Daily Mail. I loved him but was fearful of the marriage.

Late in June 1921 Gladys finally won her English Duke and became mistress of Blenheim Palace. The civil ceremony took place in a blaze

Epstein working on his sculpture of the Duke in the Undercroft at Blenheim. This work was commissioned by Gladys.

of publicity at the British Consulate in Paris on a stiflingly hot day. Her biographer relates how:

> Gladys made an early stand for the feminist cause by insisting that the word 'obey' be omitted from the responses.

She was never really happy at Blenheim. She hated the convention and formality of her life in the Palace. She missed her Continental friends. She once told Jacob Epstein, the sculptor, 'I married a house, not a man.' She was never accepted by the conservative county set who failed to understand their eccentric new neighbour. Given her bohemian background, this was perhaps understandable. In her defence, it was always going to be difficult to follow Consuelo who had been so popular with the estate

Gladys' head on a sphinx in the water terraces.

workers and local villagers. Lady Ottoline Morrell, who was a member of the Bloomsbury Group and lived nearby at Garsington, was Gladys' sole supporter, describing her as 'the only intelligent woman in Oxfordshire.'

Although not an enthusiastic participant in Sunny's beloved country sports, pheasant shooting and fox-hunting, Gladys pruned the Blenheim roses, rode in the Park and boated on the lake. She took a creative interest in Sunny's estate improvements, particularly the construction of the western water terraces. The enterprise began in 1925 under the guidance of architect, Achille Duchêne, with Gladys, a gifted amateur photographer, capturing its progress on camera. This shared adventure temporarily strengthened the marriage and earned Sunny the nickname, 'Builder Duke'. It is on these western terraces that she is immortalised at Blenheim, for Sunny placed two lead sphinxes in her distinctive image, opposite each other on the lower terrace.

There was one project in the Blenheim gardens at this time that can be attributed entirely to Gladys. In April 1924 she set about restoring the 5th Duke's rock garden at the foot of the lake behind the Cascade. Gladys spent hours single-handedly supervising the movement of rocks, the placing of steps and the building of paths. Today there is little evidence which might act as a testimony to her efforts. She had to stop work on her rock garden following a third miscarriage aged forty-four years old. A generation later, her step daughter-in-law, Mary, the 10th Duchess, buried her dachshunds in this overgrown Eden.

Gladys did make one resplendent contribution to the decoration of the Palace. In August 1928 she commissioned portrait painter, Colin

(above) Sunny surveying Gladys' rock garden at the top of the Cascade.

(left) The Cascade in full flood. Gladys' rock garden lies directly behind.

Gill, to paint her distinctive blue eyes above the main entrance. High up on the portico are six ocular panels, three blue eyes and three brown, the latter supposedly relating to Sunny.[1] Gill's whimsical work was recently restored by the 11th Duke.

In the late 1920s the relationship between Gladys and Sunny steadily deteriorated. She felt she was a prisoner in a soulless, suffocating palace with only an increasingly bad-tempered husband for company. She became desperately unhappy and yearned for her little flat in Paris. Her old friend, Walter Berry wrote: 'How can you spend all your days in Hyperboria? What are your brain cells working on?' Gladys found herself on a fast downward track. The recent economic slump had ruined her

Colin Gill painting Gladys' eyes high up under the portico.

finances. She was not taking proper care of herself and worse still, she was beginning to lose her renowned looks. Twenty-two years earlier she had injected wax into her nose to maintain her classic Grecian profile. The wax was now slipping and distorting her face. In August 1925 Lady Lee of Fareham described her as:

> Very intelligent and striking in appearance, with vivid colouring and enormous blue eyes but she is not really beautiful as she has a heavy chin which looks almost scarred and a coarse crooked mouth. She has also attempted to acquire a classic Grecian profile, by, it is said, having paraffin wax injected under her the skin of her nose but this appears to have got somewhat out of place.

*Sunny's 60th birthday celebrations. Gladys sits next to Sunny holding two of
her beloved spaniels and Winston sits on the far left of the photo. Sunny's son,
the future 10th Duke of Marlborough, stands on the far right.*

Bouts of happiness for the Marlboroughs were few and far between and
only then snatched while travelling together to France and Italy. Life at
Blenheim continued down its tedious path leaving both parties miserable
and in ill-health until finally in the summer of 1931 Sunny decamped to
his London home in Carlton House Terrace. Before the split Gladys presided over two memorable social events which would prove to be the last
public occasions when the Marlboroughs would share any happiness.
In February 1928 Gladys hosted a Leap Year Eve Ball in Carlton House
Terrace attended by many old friends in fancy dress, including the Prince
of Wales. Two years later she repeated the performance by organising a
sixtieth birthday party for Sunny at Blenheim. The festivities included a
torchlight procession to a one hundred foot high bonfire below the Monument in the Park and open air dancing in the Courtyard.

Gladys presenting the prizes at an agricultural show in Blenheim Park.

Following the separation Gladys was left alone at Blenheim with only her spaniels and a skeletal staff for company. In their loneliness both parties gravitated to animals for succour. She turned her hand to breeding pedigree Blenheim spaniels that ranged freely down the Palace's State Rooms in ever-increasing numbers. Clarissa Churchill, on a visit to Blenheim, 'was amazed to find the Great Hall divided into dog coops and reeking most terribly.' An outraged Sunny retreated to Newmarket and rekindled an interest in the Turf, enjoying no little success with a horse named Andrea which ran in the 1932 Derby and won the St James's Palace Stakes at Ascot.

In the late summer of 1933, only months before his death, Sunny finally regained his Palace. Gladys, after a short spell in London, retired into the obscurity of the Northamptonshire countryside, only to be rediscovered by Hugo Vickers in a local mental hospital some forty years later. Why did their relationship go so horribly wrong? There were, of course, faults on both sides. She was disillusioned by life at Blenheim. She was a bohemian intellectual trapped in a dull, oppressive, over-bearing, provincial world. Her exciting existence living in Paris and travelling the

Sunny at the races. He loved horses and enjoyed a lifelong interest in the 'Turf'.

Continent as a Duke's mistress must have seemed a lifetime away. One must assume that Sunny was a different man at home in Oxfordshire. His responsibilities as a Duke, landlord, tenant of a Palace and Lord Lieutenant weighed heavily on his shoulders. He must have been particularly difficult to live with. Gladys constantly referred to his temper and how Sunny changed radically after his conversion to Catholicism, becoming a more distant, spiritual person. The sad irony remains that while no tenant of the Palace, with the exception of the 4th Duke, has done more to cherish and embellish Blenheim than Sunny, his Duchess, Gladys, a woman of extraordinary beauty, wit and intellect, is only remembered for her deep blue eyes and Grecian profile. For one so gifted, surely hers was an unfulfilled life?

9

The Duke's final years and death

In the years before his death on 30 June 1934, Sunny spent much of his time in London where his home was in the elegant Carlton House Terrace. His appointment diary for 1932 was reasonably full, being entertained by such friends as Lady Curzon, the Duchess of Roxburghe and Lady Queensbury. The month of March started with the entry 'Dancing at the Savoy'. All his life he had enjoyed dancing and in April he started having rumba lessons. He once said: 'Dancing is the finest exercise. It makes old men young and graceful.' Clearly he was not averse to this more racy dancing style and his health was good enough at this point to dance.

Sunny supported, largely through eating fine dinners, a number of societies during 1932 and the choice of charities and societies reflected not just his sense of duty, but also his faith and his personal interests. In March he dined with the Society of Miniature Painters. In October he attended a dinner in aid of the Mission to Seamen at the Mansion House. Early in November he dined at the Holburn Restaurant with the Westminster Catholic Federation and later on 17 November, he attended the Primrose League Banquet at the Hotel Metropole. December saw him attend the Annual Banquet of the Incorporated Association of Architects and Surveyors. It was fortunate that he appreciated a good dinner.

One of the sad tasks Sunny had to perform in 1932 was to unveil a bust of the late Lord Birkenhead in the Debating Hall of the Oxford Union Society on 4 November. His great friend F.E. had died of pneumonia on 30 September 1930. That these two men should ever have been friends was most unlikely given their different backgrounds. Sunny,

*The Duke, not in the best of health, but still out and about with his son
and heir, John Albert, who was known as Bert.*

however, became friends with F.E. long before he had climbed to the
very top of his professional ladder and had been ennobled as Lord Birkenhead. He and F.E. had been firm friends since their twenties, despite
the fact that F.E. was loud, opinionated and supremely confident. As
Winston wrote:

Perhaps no two men could have been more utterly dis-similar – the Duke reserved and precise; FE reckless and audacious. Yet they loved one another. They had… certain qualities in common, in particular, a lion hearted courage and a passion for horses.

The Duke did not neglect Blenheim even though he spent more of his time in London. By 1932 Mr Sacre was the Duke's land agent.[1] Mr Sacre came up to London for meetings and caught up with Sunny on the relatively few occasions when he came back up to Oxfordshire. Sunny went back for such matters as meetings in the Woodstock Town Hall, the Annual Cricket Club meeting and the time when the National Art Collection Fund Association visited the Palace.

Bert was married to Alexandra Mary Cadogan, a daughter of Viscount Chelsea. They married in 1920. In this photograph Mary and Bert are both seated. They had five children. John, who became the 11th Duke of Marlborough, Charles, Sarah, Caroline and Rosemary. Caroline was the mother of Michael Waterhouse, co-author of this book.

Three of Sunny's grandchildren, Sarah, John and Caroline, in the Park at Blenheim.

1933 saw far fewer social engagements in Sunny's diary and repeated references to appointments with his doctor. Clearly he was not in robust health. He made only a few visits to Blenheim, once for the visit in July of fifty members of the Royal Empire Society and again when his friends Mr and Mrs McGrath came to stay in September.

The early months of 1934 followed the same quiet pattern, with the exception that in February he went on a Catholic retreat for a few days. He had been admitted to the Catholic faith on 1 February 1927 after three years of instruction by the Jesuit Priest, Father Martindale. Sunny had always been a spiritual man, as acknowledged by his cousin Winston Churchill who wrote in the Duke's obituary that he needed some form of contact with the 'sublime and supernatural'. Winston intimated that his cousin's deep unhappiness drove him towards the Catholic Church. When Sunny asked to be admitted to this faith, his request was granted, but only after lengthy preparation and consideration.

The Catholic Church, at this time, was a much more forgiving institution than the inflexible and dogmatic Anglican Church.[2] Before his conversion to the Catholic faith, Sunny had supported the established

Anglican Church both by his attendance and patronage; the Bladon and Woodstock Benefice were in 'his gift'. The rift with the Anglican Church came after his divorce in 1921. In October 1922 the Bishop of Oxford stated that Sunny could not attend the Oxford Diocesan conference on the grounds that he could no longer take communion in the Church of England. The Bishop did not go on to say why he could no longer take communion but everyone knew it was because Sunny was a divorcee. He had not declared his intention of going to the conference so the Bishop's words were a pre-emptive strike. Perhaps it was the Bishop's attack that forced him to reconsider his position as a 'non-communicant' of the Anglican Church, a position he found unsatisfactory. He then approached the Catholic Church and was introduced to Father Martindale who launched him into a period of study that lasted as long as most people take to study for a degree.

Historically the Spencer-Churchill family had always been followers of the established Church so it was unusual for him to even consider conversion to the Catholic faith. He was not a stranger to the Catholic faith, however. There were Catholics within his family. His cousin, Jack Churchill was married to a most devout Catholic, Lady Gwendoline Bertie, daughter of the 7th Earl of Abingdon. Sunny was very fond of Gwendoline and she, along with her family, was a frequent visitor to Blenheim. Another friend, relation and frequent visitor to the Palace was Shane Leslie, who was also a Catholic convert. So there were familial reasons to look towards the Catholic faith. Also a short distance from the Palace, at Begbroke, stood a Catholic monastery which was part of the Priory of St Philip. This was a novitiate house. There is an unsubstantiated story that Sunny actually first met Father Martindale whilst out walking near the monastery. There is no evidence for this rather serendipitous scenario but he and Father Martindale did become close friends during the three years of study. When he was finally admitted to the Catholic Faith, Gwendoline was one of those who witnessed the event, as did his second wife Gladys. She herself claimed that her parents had her baptised in both the Protestant and Catholic faiths, to cover all eventualities. For the remainder of his life Sunny was, as Winston said, 'fortified' by his Catholic faith.

Having returned to London in February 1934 after his retreat, Sunny's social calendar was very quiet until June when there was a flurry of seeing friends. Two of his last public commitments took him back to Blenheim on Saturday 16 June to give out Prizes for the Competition of Bands and to open the new church in Woodstock on the Sunday. He then returned to London and there were no further entries in his diary.

Sunny died of cancer on 30 July 1934 at 7 Carlton House Terrace in London. Typical of the man, he had left instructions that the servants at Carlton House Terrace were to be paid for a month after his death and given time to find another place. Carlton House Terrace was rented and therefore the servants could not automatically transfer to the employ of the 10th Duke. Mr Sacre was quick to reassure the servants by writing to Alice Hodson, the housekeeper at Carlton House Terrace, that the servants were not to worry about leaving immediately. The Duke was mindful of his servants' welfare to the end. This care extended far beyond those who served him directly. Of the many kind words written about him after he died, one of the points made in *The Times* was his exemplary care of those who lived on his Estate and worked for him. The newspaper said the 9th Duke:

> had devoted himself to the care of his Estates and the people on them. Among his tenants he was regarded as an ideal landlord, and one to whom they could always go for advice with the knowledge that all that was possible would be done to further their interests.

On the last evening of his life Sunny held a tea party for those who were dear to him. Winston was one of those invited and he said that his cousin fell asleep after talking with his friends for most of the evening. He did not wake up again. Later Winston wrote:

> He knew quite well that his end was approaching, that he was, as he said, at the end of his tether. He faced this universal ordeal with dignity and simplicity, making neither too much nor too little of it.

Sunny had made the arrangements for his own funeral ten years before he died. On 12 June 1924 he engaged Messrs. W. Garstin & Sons Ltd, funeral directors, of 49 Wigmore Street, Cavendish Square, London. It is not known if he was in ill health at the time. Certainly in the autumn of 1925 he saw his London doctor quite regularly. His main doctor was Dr

THE DUKE'S FINAL YEARS AND DEATH

Matthews but he also saw a Dr Gibson. Letters in the Blenheim archives make it clear he was having some sort of treatment but do not say what for. In one letter to Dr Matthews Sunny wrote:

> Dr. Gibson has already given me a dose and he will report progress to you at a later date. I presume you will tell Dr. Gibson when to increase the doses. At present I feel no ill effects.

Perhaps this was the beginning of his battle against cancer or perhaps it was the sciatica that plagued him from time to time.

The 9th Duke of Marlborough's funeral service took place in two parts, first in London at the Church of the Immaculate Conception in Farm Street and the second at the Monastery in Begbroke, near the Palace.[3] In London the service was conducted by Father Stewart, Father D'Arcy, Father Devas, Father Martindale and Cardinal Bourne. The Church was full with family and friends, Dukes, Marquesses, Earls, Viscounts, Lords and Ladies and many old friends, including the artist Paul Maze, whose paintings hang in the Palace to this day. Society came out in force to say goodbye. Sunny had been born in India and the Continent of his birth was represented by the Maharajah of Burdwan. Members of the Royal family did not attend the service but the King was represented by the Marquess of Salisbury.

Many of the mourners followed the coffin to Blenheim for the second part of the funeral service, which was lead by Father Martindale. Some time before he died Sunny gave a copy of the poem 'Dark Night' by St John of the Cross to Father Martindale with the request that it be read 'over his grave'. Father Martindale read the poem in Blenheim Chapel as the coffin was lowered into the crypt.

His coffin had come up by train from London and was drawn by Estate horses to the Monastery and then to Blenheim Chapel. During this part of the service Father Martindale spoke of Sunny's profound faith and his indomitable courage. He had believed that suffering was part of Christian life and so morphine had only been administered after he had lost consciousness. Father Martindale said: 'I think he was for only one complete day in bed.' The priest also spoke of Sunny's strong sense of order, discipline and his firmly held belief that, 'with privilege went responsibility'. Clearly Father Martindale had known Sunny well.

The crypt lies underneath the floor in Blenheim Chapel. There Sunny was laid to rest next to his ancestors.

As the funeral cortege moved slowly from the Monastery through Woodstock and the Park, the family members who followed on foot noticed that shops were shut, curtains were drawn and local people lined the route. The Duke's gardeners formed a guard of honour around the horse-drawn hearse as it went through the Park and upon reaching Blenheim Chapel, the gamekeepers acted as pallbearers. Sunny, in accordance with his wishes, was interred in the vault underneath the Chapel, alongside his ancestors, including John Churchill, the 1st Duke of Marlborough.

There were several obituaries written about him in the newspapers of the day. They commented on his interest in agriculture, the welfare of his tenants and his determination to maintain the glory of Blenheim. In the *Sunday Express* Lord Castlerosse could not resist speaking ill of the dead. He wrote:

To me he was a pathetic figure like a lonely peacock struggling through deserted gardens... The Duke of Marlborough was the last Duke who firmly believed that strawberry leaves could... cover a multitude of sins.

Harsh words indeed! The Duke's cousin and great friend Winston took an altogether more balanced approach when he wrote his obituary in *The Times*. This fair assessment was acknowledged by Ivor, Sunny's younger son, who wrote to Winston to thank him for his kind words. Ivor wrote:

I cannot tell you what a tower of strength and what a fountain of wisdom you are on the big occasions in life. Of all the final words that were offered to my father, yours touched us the most and will be a continual consolation. I have read your tribute several times and will do so many more and I feel it will give pleasure to all those who, like myself, strive to understand without criticising and to appreciate without adulation.

The last word should then be left to Winston Churchill:

At first sight the 9th Duke seemed too small, too frail, for those grave and stately titles that he bore. But on closer acquaintance they became him superbly for the dignity of his bearing, the formality of his manner, were always more striking than the smallness of his stature... He will ever remain in the memory of his guests, a generous and delightful host... The Duke died as he lived, a brave man and a great gentleman.

Epilogue

History has been unkind to Sunny Marlborough. He has not been depicted as a popular and attractive figure. A major reason must be that his story thus far has been written through the eyes of two unhappy and broken marriages. True, he was at times difficult to fathom and had a complex character moulded during a miserable childhood. He was born to be small and slight in stature giving an appearance of weakness and fragility and, not surprisingly, as he matured, he lacked the confidence and showmanship of his charismatic younger cousin, Winston Churchill.

To those who did not know him well he could give the impression of being distant, melancholic, pompous and self-important. Sunny's almost feudal sense of pride in his position proved time and again to be an unfortunate side to his personality. He was adept at upsetting even the closest members of his family. He never forgave his father for disgracing the family name, in addition to selling Blenheim's unique picture collection. He could not bring himself to admit that it was a profusion of American dollars which had facilitated his construction projects and lavish lifestyle at Blenheim and at Sunderland House in London. This seems both rude and grossly unfair to his ultra-generous father-in-law, William K. Vanderbilt, and his likeable and supportive step-mother, Lilian Hammersley, who was responsible for so many of Blenheim's improvements in the late 1880's. As with so many of his ilk at this time he was unable to accept that Americans, and indeed women in general, were his equals.

To the new liberal elite in Britain Sunny no doubt appeared to be a sad upholder of an ancient order, that after the seismic changes wrought by the Parliament Act and the First World War, had shattered around him. The power of the aristocracy had been emasculated during the prime of his life. Although an intelligent, politically aware individual, he found it difficult to come to terms with the modern world as exemplified by the Labour Party and their Trade Union allies. Winston wrote in Sunny's obituary:

> He was always conscious that he belonged to a system which had been destroyed, to a society that had passed away. He resigned himself to this but it cast a shadow on his life.

To his close group of heavyweight friends who knew and loved him well, he came across as an altogether different individual, blessed with many and varied special qualities. Muriel Wilson wrote to Winston about Sunny on his death:

> Oh yes, he was whimsical and difficult to understand but what rare qualities he had and only those, alas, who loved him really realised them.

Discerning commentators such as Winston and F.E. Smith described him as the model aristocrat, generous, clever, courteous, patriotic, sensitive, erudite, artistic and charming. As demonstrated through his relationships with his first cousins, Winston Churchill and Ivor Guest, he was at heart a devoted family man. It was his inspiration that large family Christmases became an institution at Blenheim. He was also a kind and fair landlord who invariably displayed an indomitable sense of duty whether it be in connection with his estate, county or country. At Sunny's funeral in the Palace chapel Father Martindale gave a tribute to the Duke and stated:

> Yet I insist, and with a certain obstinacy, that he was sure that with privilege went responsibility: a name, a Palace, a rank were not mere instruments for self-indulgence.

Ian Malcolm, a Conservative politician and close Churchill family friend, said of Sunny: 'He had a heart of gold hidden behind bad health and a disappointed temperament.' Sunny achieved much in his lifetime, not only at Blenheim but also in fulfilling his public duties. The 'disappointed temperament' almost certainly stems from the failure of his two marriages. He was particularly affected by his acrimonious break-up from Consuelo that attracted so much bad publicity on both sides of the Atlantic. In addition he had to suffer ostracism from the Court. For a man who had only a few years earlier been the most favoured aristocrat in the land and who cared passionately about the good name of the Spencer-Churchill family, this was hard to bear. With his father's repudiation by the Establishment never far away from his thoughts, this was simply another sad chapter in his recent family history repeating itself.

It is at Blenheim that Sunny will be best remembered. He saw it as his duty to protect and enrich the Palace together with its surrounding Estate. Surely no steward, except perhaps the 4th Duke who commissioned 'Capability' Brown, has been so successful in his life's mission. Sunny inherited an estate that had suffered from generations of under-investment and family finances that were near bankruptcy. He married one of the richest heiresses in the world but at a great personal cost. He sacrificed a lifetime's happiness for a Palace he loved deeply. He was proud to be its steward and was determined at his death to leave it in a better state than when he inherited it. It is surely fair to say that in being so successful with such endeavours, this perfectionist Duke, backed by Consuelo's material resources, together with his own energy, vision and educated taste, saved Blenheim both for his family and the nation.

Notes

Chapter 1

1. A. L. Rowse, *The Later Churchills*, (London, 1958), p.272.

Chapter 2

1. The 11th Duke of Marlborough, grandson of the 9th Duke, named one of his dogs, Jerry.
2. Sir H. Drummond-Wolff was Ambassador in Madrid 1892-1900.
3. He died in 1934. Her book, *The Glitter and the Gold* was published in 1953 so there was no opportunity for the Duke to reply or defend himself.
4. Albertha's father and the Duke's grandfather.
5. The Undercroft was the lowest floor of the Palace where the servants' working rooms were. It was not underground just underneath all the other floors.
6. There was a florist, as there is today, to arrange the flowers for the main rooms in the Palace and Consuelo's bedroom.

Chapter 3

1. (In church use) a position as a vicar or rector with an income or property.

Chapter 4

1. Just before the war four members of the Hollis family worked in the Palace.

Chapter 5

1. The fountains in the Chapel Terrace, the upper terrace, were added later by the 9th Duke's son, Bert the 10th Duke.
2. A caryatid is a sculpted form, usually female, which can take the place of a supporting column in a building or as in this case can serve as an architectural feature on a retaining wall. The caryatids on the Water Terraces echo those on the west front of the Palace.
3. The term Boulle relates to a form of inlaid furniture decoration usually composed of brass and tortoiseshell. Andre Boulle was a French cabinet maker who reached the height of his fame during the reign of Queen Anne.

Chapter 6

1. In 1886 the Liberal Party had split over Home Rule for Ireland and Joseph Chamberlain, together with the Duke of Devonshire, formed the Liberal Unionist Party. They and ninety-four other Liberal Unionist Members of Parliament established a political alliance with the Conservative Party in opposition to Irish Home Rule.
2. He had been made a Privy Councillor in 1899.

Chapter 7

1. It is interesting that in 1955 Churchill was offered and refused the Dukedom of London. Accepting the peerage would have cut short a career in the Commons for his son Randolph.
2. The Clerical Tithes Bill which upset the Non-Conformist Liberal vote.
3. Claque refers to a group of sycophants.
4. B. Johnson, *The Churchill Factor: How One Man Made History* (London, 2014), p.156.
5. The other was Lord Birkenhead who died on 30 September 1930.

Chapter 8

1. An American newspaper reported that Sunny had blue eyes.

Chapter 9

1. Mr Sacre would stay on and serve the 10th Duke after Sunny died.
2. Father Julian of the Brompton Oratory rather charmingly described the Catholic Church to Sunny's great grandson as 'a field hospital.'
3. The Monastery buildings are now used as a school for children with special educational needs.

Index

References

We acknowledge with gratitude the work of the many authors who have, before us, researched and written about the fascinating story of Blenheim and the Spencer-Churchills. References include but are not limited to the following:

The Blenheim Archives

The Archival papers and photographs of Gladys Deacon, courtesy of Hugo Vickers

Gladys, Duchess of Marlborough by Hugo Vickers

Consuelo & Alva Vanderbilt by Amanda Mackenzie Stuart

The Glitter & the Gold by Consuelo Vanderbilt Balsan

Blenheim & the Churchill Family by Henrietta Spencer-Churchill

From Winston with Love and Kisses by Celia Sandys

The Churchills by David Green

Blenheim Palace by David Green

The Churchills by Mary S. Lovell

Winston As I Knew Him by Violet Bonham Carter

Jennie: The Mother of Winston Churchill by Anita Leslie

Lily, Duchess of Marlborough by Sally Svenson

Blenheim: Biography of a Palace by Marian Fowler

Churchill's Grandmama: Frances 7th Duchess of Marlborough by Margaret Elizabeth Forster

Blenheim: Landscape for a Palace edited by James Bond & Kate Tiller

The Finest View in England – The Landscape and Gardens at Blenheim Palace by Jeri Bapasola

The Churchill Factor by Boris Johnson

The Oxfordshire Hussars in the Great War by Adrian Keith-Falconer

Blenheim Revisited: The Spencer-Churchills and their Palace by Hugh Montgomery-Massingberd

Acknowledgements

His Grace, the Duke of Marlborough
The Blenheim Trustees
Hugo Vickers
SOFO
Country Life
Oxfordshire County Archives
Churchill family / Curtis Brown
Houses of Parliament Archives
The late Lady Juliet Townsend and the descendants of F.E.Smith
Mrs Alexa Frost, Archivist at Blenheim Palace
Mr Richard Cragg, photographer
Churchill Archives, Churchill College, Cambridge